Self, Made

Fourteen Modern Artists from the Richard and Ellen Sandor Family Collection

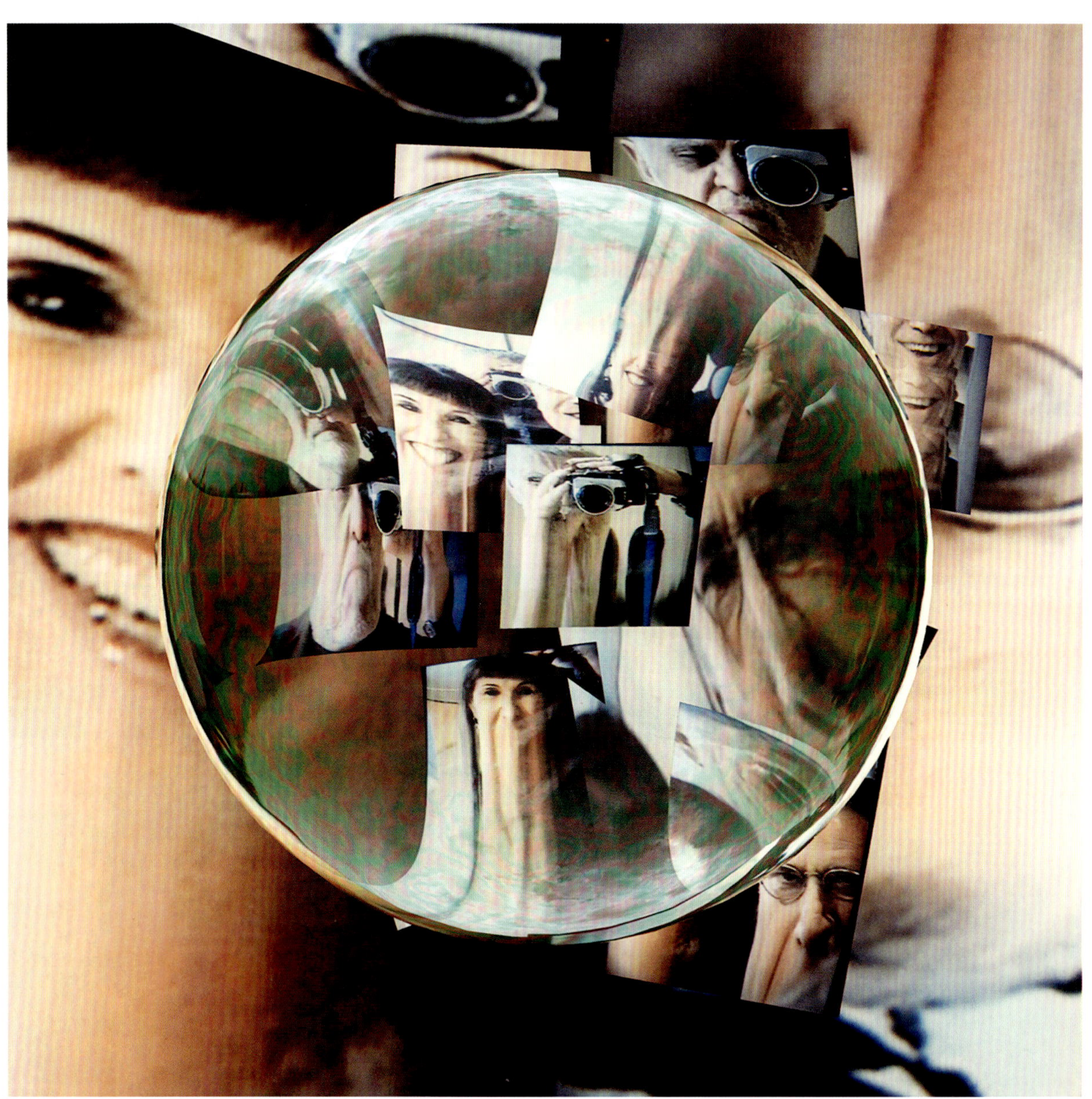

Self, Made

Fourteen Modern Artists from the Richard and Ellen Sandor Family Collection

Matthew S. Witkovsky

The Art Institute of Chicago

Distributed by
Yale University Press
New Haven and
London

Contents

Artists and Artworks

Foreword

Dialogues between academically trained makers and those labeled as "self-taught," "outsider" or, more recently, "outlier" artists have long had a place in collections and exhibitions at the Art Institute of Chicago. Paths to visibility for the latter group of makers came through the activities of 1960s graduates of the School of the Art Institute of Chicago (SAIC), loosely known as the Chicago School, whose work has been championed at the museum and who in turn have shone a light on their peers working independently of academic art centers. The museum's Arts of the Americas and Textiles departments have long promoted African American artists grounded in folk or community traditions, centering these makers' connections to Chicago.

Since the 1970s Richard and Ellen Sandor have brought these dialogues into their Chicago apartment, and to one room in particular—a room they have referred to with sincerity and respect as the "Outsider Café," whose contents debut to the public in the museum's Modern Wing. In their collection, Ellen, herself an SAIC alum and a practicing artist, and Richard, an economist by day and photography sleuth and historian by night, have juxtaposed works by legendary "outsiders"—William Edmondson, Lee Godie, Bill Traylor, and Eugene Von Bruenchenhein, among others—with select examples of art by academically trained artists such as Cindy Sherman and Kara Walker.

The richness of those many connections makes for a singularly dynamic and fertile exhibition organized by Matthew S. Witkovsky, the Richard and Ellen Sandor Chair and Curator of Photography and Media. Matt emphatically shares the Sandors' understanding of photography as an expansive field in which professionally trained and self-taught makers have always rubbed shoulders. Struggles for recognition by individual photographers and debates about the cultural or artistic merit of photographs as such have shaped the history of this field and continue today. Rather than try to settle such debates, the department of Photography and Media insists—as the Sandors have long done—on multiplicity and heterogeneity as the necessary grounding for a truly creative society.

The Sandors' installation in their home constituted such a society in microcosm. Now, thanks to the gifts of art illustrated in this book, their vision is reaching the widest possible audience and entering a far larger and lasting home. We are grateful to Ellen and Richard Sandor for sharing these artists' works with our audiences.

James Rondeau
President and Eloise W. Martin Director
The Art Institute of Chicago

Preface and Acknowledgments

This exhibition has three curators: Ellen Sandor, Richard Sandor, and myself. It was the Sandors who established the basic checklist of works, nearly all of which are drawn from a room in their Chicago apartment that they filled progressively from about 1980 through the early 2000s with a variety of pieces whose makers, having developed their talents outside art schools and gallery or museum networks, were known in the art world as "outsiders." In the conversation that follows on pages 12 to 25, Richard and Ellen make clear their own self-awareness as outsiders: Brooklyn transplants in Minneapolis, Berkeley, and Chicago; supporters of rights for the incarcerated; admirers of innovation rooted in antiestablishment thinking. Proud contrarians, they understandably feel at home with artists who assert their individuality separate from or even against the "art system."

Responding to the Sandors' convictions, I organized the show around selfhood as something that an individual (re)-defines in dialogue with others and in tandem with societal shifts and constraints. Self, made. The framework is far from novel or profound, but it is eminently useful. For one, it casts selfhood as *made* rather than *given*, and in doing so implies self-construction as an effort or a challenge—often a considerable one. If art seems hard to make well or successfully, consider how much harder it can be to make one's self, especially if the identity in question lies conspicuously "outside the norm."

In a related way, I hoped with this title to present the makers in this book as individual selves and thereby to underscore that it is the curators who have joined them in conversation with one another: as at a party with a boldly varied guest list. Indeed, following the Sandors' terrific model of a café setting, I imagined the exhibition gallery as a room in animated conversation whose earnest, engaging buzz draws newcomers inside. (Inside, not outside.) The image is quaint or, as the three of us would say, *haimish*, but it is meant sincerely.

In the name of my fellow hosts, I extend our deepest appreciation to all those who have helped to organize this gathering. Janine Fron and Iris Chaoui-Boudrane at the Sandor Family Collection have smoothed the way at every step. Jamie Stukenberg made the outstanding photographs of the Sandors, their artworks, and their museum-like residence on North Astor, and Robert Chase Heishman and Robert Salazar crafted a video to match. At the Art Institute, Julia Loughlin in Collections and Loans supervised the transport of delicate artworks with appropriate care. These attentions were paired with visits from conservators Haddon Dine, Emily Mercer, and Katrina Rush, who all worked mightily to ready the objects for photography and display, along with Felice Robles, Mardy Sears, and Andrew Talley.

Briana Gonzalez in Exhibitions and Jamie Vaught-Karasek in Photography and Media tackled all of these preparatory steps and much other organizational work; they both took on the numerous complexities of this checklist with typically unflappable dedication. Bri and Jamie also coordinated with Bonnie Rosenberg in Imaging and photographers Nathan Keay, Robert Lifson, Jonathan Mathias, Juan Molina Hernández, and Joe Tallarico, who worked at lightning speed to make the book's many and varied photographs. Elyse M. Allen with Kaitlyn Fultz-Campion and Hayley Hinsberger handled pre- and postproduction. Those images form part of a publishing effort that, in making the Sandors' Chicago apartment feel "at home" at the Art Institute, has been the main driver of the project. Great thanks go to the team in Publishing, first-rate as always: David Khan-Giordano oversaw production; Nora McGreevy edited the text; and Kristie Kahns sourced and obtained copyright for images; all with help from Lauren Makholm, Lisa Meyerowitz, Katie Reilly, and Isella Sandoval. Cheryl Towler Weese, J. Brad Sturm, and Meredith Barone of Studio Blue, Chicago, crafted a design for the book that elegantly brings the past into the present and endows it with new resonances. Further thanks are warmly extended to the many colleagues who collaborated to tend to these works, design and build the exhibition, and make it safe, engaging, and accessible: Megan Creamer, Marielle Epstein, Erin Clark Fenton, Annette Gaspers, James Iska, Kelly Keegan, Kari McCluskey, Haiqa Nisar, Thomas Ryan, Becca Schlossberg, Layne Thue-Bludworth, and Lucio Ventura.

The Sandors and I offer thanks to the chairs of curatorial departments who, alongside Photography and Media, will steward their generous gifts: Kevin Salatino in Prints and Drawings, Sarah Kelly Oehler in Arts of the Americas, and Paulina Pobocha in Modern and Contemporary Art. We are grateful above all to the museum leadership that shapes and promotes exhibition undertakings at the Art Institute, including Sarah Guernsey, Deputy Director and Senior Vice President for Curatorial Affairs; Sarah Kelly Oehler, Field-McCormick Chair and Curator, Arts of the Americas, and Vice President of Curatorial Strategy; David Nacol, Senior Vice President, Philanthropy; Katie Rahn, Senior Vice President, Marketing and Communications; Emily Benedict, Vice President, Campus Operations; Amy Allen, Vice President, Engagement; Aaron Andersen, Associate Vice President, Financial Planning and Analysis; and foremost the President and Eloise W. Martin Director of the Art Institute of Chicago, James Rondeau.

Appreciation for authorial permissions and artist conversations goes to Allison Calhoun, Víctor Espinosa, Yolanda Jones, Annette Messager, Arthur Roger, Kara Walker, and John Waters. The last sentence of thanks is reserved, meanwhile, for my patrons, co-curators, and good friends: Richard and Ellen Sandor. You have welcomed me into your marvelous homes and your life together, and you have shown me how extraordinary it can be to live as one with each other and with art.

Matthew S. Witkovsky
Richard and Ellen Sandor Chair and Curator, Photography and Media
Vice President for Strategic Art Initiatives
The Art Institute of Chicago

With love and gratitude to our family: Dr. Julie Sandor, Penya Sandor, Jack Ludden, Eric Taub, Elijah Sandor-Ludden, Justine Sandor-Ludden, Caleb Sandor-Taub, Oscar Sandor-Taub, and Dr. Jeffrey Simon.

For their kindred spirits and friendship in all things art, and for being there with us from the beginning: James Zanzi and Lisa Stone; Rick and Joann Ferina.

For their assistance with the general routine, practical needs, and care of the collection: Mariana Schiop, Robert Egan, David Auxier, Ryan Davies and his team.

For their research and attention to detail with regards to featured works in the exhibition: William Channing; Rhonda Brewer, Pecos National Historical Park; Kathleen Lamb; Shari Cavin; and Gretchen Burch.

In memory of the late great Carl Hammer, Brent Sikkema, Mr. Imagination, and James Prinz, who are with us in the spirit of being "Self, Made." For all the featured artists, for taking risks, being authentic, and sharing their unique visions as stakeholders in the future of our world. We are equally grateful for these and many more colleagues and friends who have been with us on our exciting journey in exploring and collecting art.

Richard and Ellen Sandor

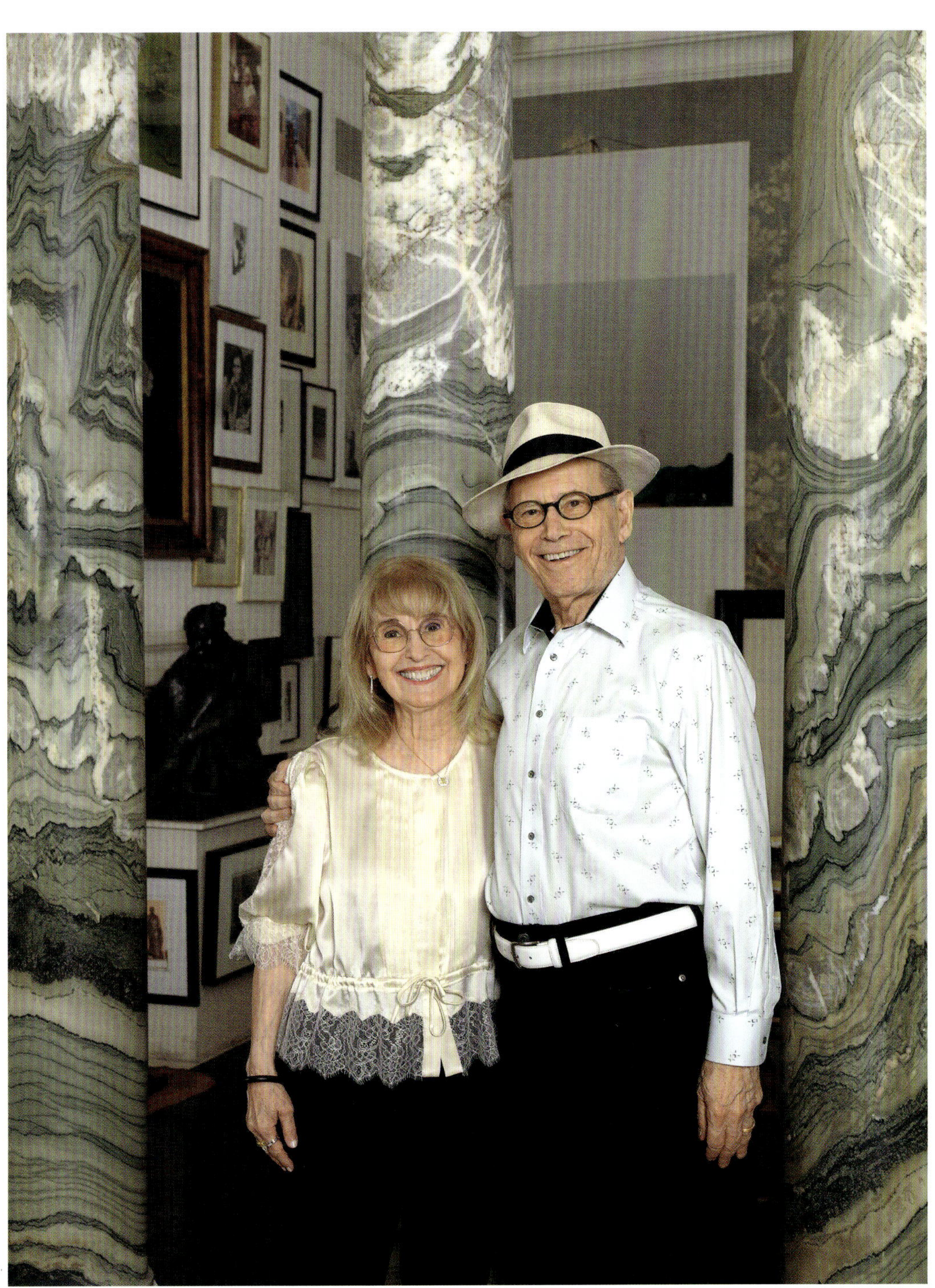

Friday, May 16, 2025 at the Chicago home of Richard and Ellen Sandor

On Art and Innovation

Richard and Ellen Sandor in Conversation with Matthew S. Witkovsky

Matthew S. Witkovsky *Let's start, if it's not too obvious, with beginnings. You moved from Berkeley to Chicago in 1972. When did you get this apartment?*

Richard and Ellen Sandor
In 1977 — but we moved in at the start of 1978. It was our primary residence from then until four years ago, when we moved to Sarasota.

The first photograph you purchased was Breakfast Room at Belle Grove Plantation *by Walker Evans. When did you buy it and where were you living at the time?*

Richard
We bought it in 1977.

Same time as you bought the apartment.

Both
Right!

Richard
Look at the *Plantation* photograph (fig. 1). It's got the columns, same as the Potter Palmer columns in the apartment.

Ellen
Jim Zanzi [a key mentor then teaching at the School of the Art Institute of Chicago (SAIC)] said, "You won't believe this," and showed it to Richard, and we said, "Oh, it's so perfect." Very literal, but perfect.

Richard
We came with one other piece and that was Auguste Rodin's *Man with Broken Nose* (fig. 2).

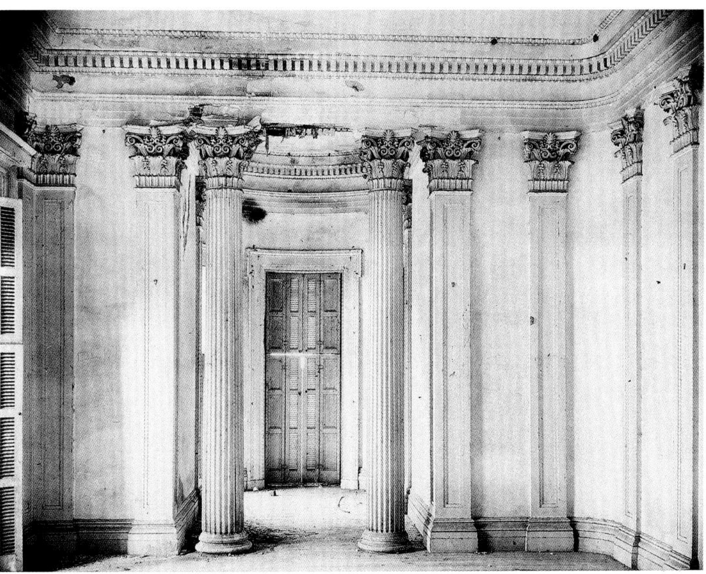

Figure 1 Walker Evans (born St. Louis, 1903; died New Haven, CT, 1975), *Breakfast Room at Belle Grove Plantation, White Chapel, Louisiana*, 1935, printed 1974. Gelatin silver print; 25.9 × 32.8 cm (10 ¼ × 12 15⁄16 in.). Collection of Richard and Ellen Sandor.

Figure 2 Auguste Rodin (born Paris, 1840; died Meudon, France, 1917), *Masque de l'Homme au nez cassé* (*Man with Broken Nose*), 1863, cast posthumously. Bronze; 47 × 19.7 × 14 cm (18½ × 7¾ × 5½ in.). Collection of Richard and Ellen Sandor.

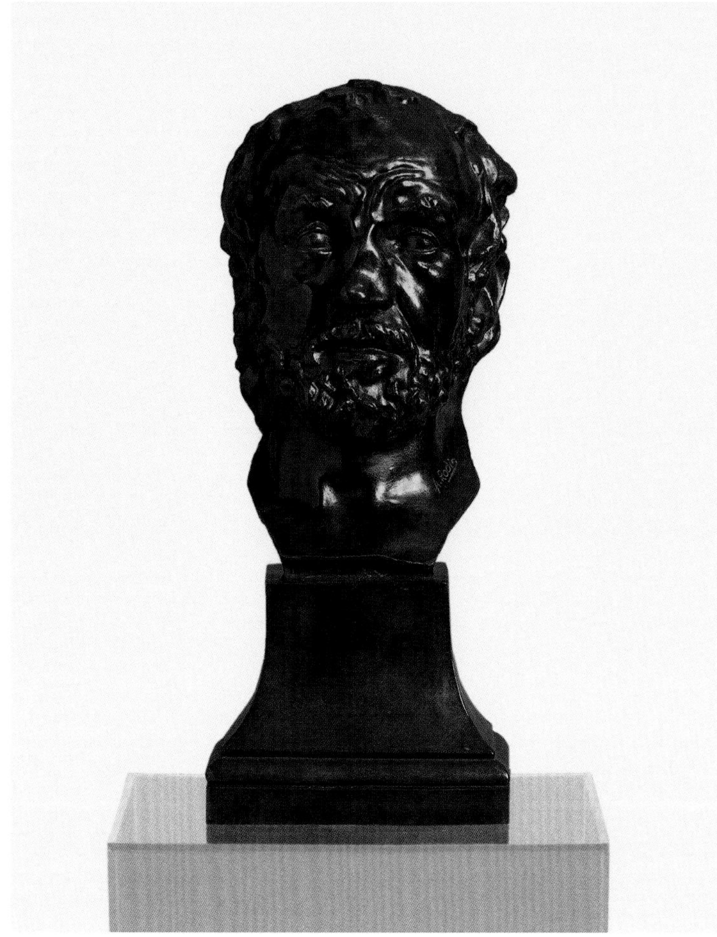

Because Ellen is a sculptor?

Richard
Not exactly, or only in part. The story is that I left the Board of Trade in 1975 and became a financial futures broker. And one of my first customers was a man by the name of Bernie Cantor.

Aha — the founder of Cantor Fitzgerald and benefactor of the Rodin-rich Cantor Sculpture Garden at Stanford University, in Palo Alto, near to where you had been teaching.

Richard
He said, "I'm your customer and friend, and I want to educate you, and you need to buy Rodin." He told me the story of his own journey into art collecting and Rodin's central place in that journey.

Ellen
And why this piece in particular, because it's the forerunner to modern sculpture. A giant innovation in art. Let's just say Richard and I are very comfortable with innovation.

The search for innovation is a key motivator in your art making and art purchases. Innovation and a personal connection.

Richard
It just flowed together.

Ellen
Back to the apartment — we came to see it, and very quickly we moved in. Suzy Morton Davidson was living here; she's the child pictured on Morton salt. How it happened was, I recommended Richard join the Board of the SAIC. I was a neon artist at the time. I was pretty wild. We had rented an apartment at Lake Point Tower that had shag carpeting. One work that I had made [while studying] at the Art Institute, called *Brooklyn*, was our breakfast table, and our coffee table was called *California*, inspired by the outsider artists of Wisconsin.[1] We had neon signs on the wall, mattresses on the floor. When Richard realized we had to leave in ninety days because the lease was nearly up…

Richard
…three- or four-months' time. It was the end of summer 1977…

Ellen
…he's really good at pinpointing things, so he sees a real estate ad, what did it say?

Richard
It said, "One of the five best apartments" —

Ellen
— "Art Deco masterpiece!" —

Richard
— "in the city of Chicago." But it was a blind ad, no address, just a phone number…

Ellen
…so I call up, and if you think my accent is Brooklyn now, you can imagine: "Hello? I wanna see the apartment." And she answers: "Yes, *dahling*…" and then, "wait a minute, are you the neon artist? And your charming husband, is he on the Board of the School?"

Getting Richard on that Board was one of the best things you ever did!

Ellen
Right. I walk into the apartment and all I did was scream. Suzy asks what I think of this or that, and I'm just screaming my delight. I tell her that I love every single thing about it, the only problem is that we don't have any money. Everything else is perfect! She asked to bring Richard around, so I called his office and explained he needed to leave immediately and come to see this place unless he wanted a divorce. And that's how we got the apartment.

Richard
The President of the Board of the Art Institute of Chicago at that time, Larry Chalmers, lived in this building as well.

Figure 3 The "Outsider Café" in the Sandor family apartment.

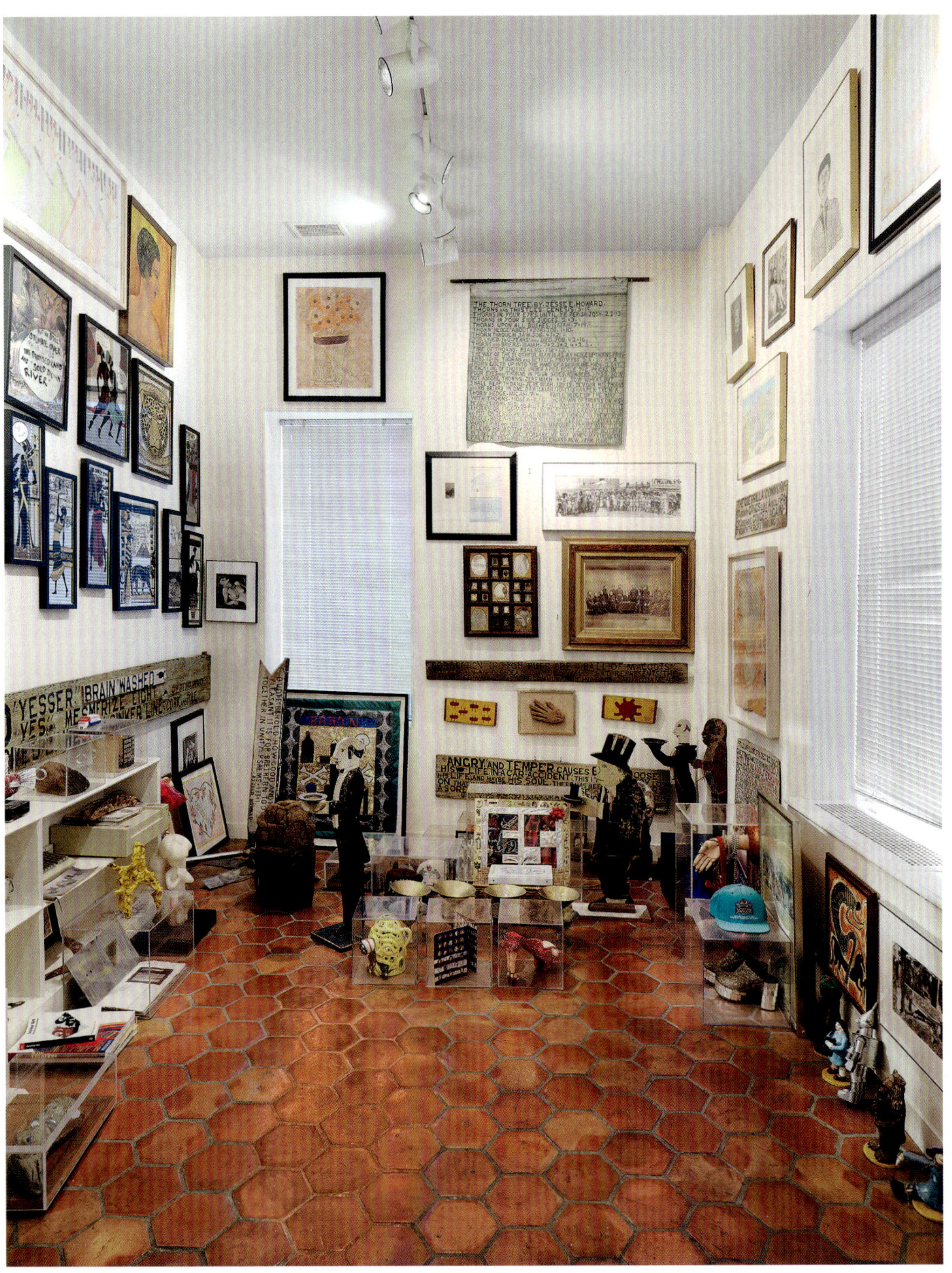

We moved in with two kids in tow, the photograph by Walker Evans, and the Rodin. And not a stick of furniture.

This empty place beckoned the art. And self-taught artists, as Sidney Janis influentially called them, were among the first you welcomed into this home.[2] Is that right?

Ellen

I was on the board of Intuit.[3] Jim Zanzi got me looking at self-taught work — along with several women for whom this kind of art was a passion.

In interviews you've explained your flair for innovation and the new; Richard, meanwhile, you bring the historian's eye and a dedication to research. Self-taught artists can seem to operate against these priorities; they might appear to embody an almost anti-modern individuality, preferring drawing or painting to technological media, and insisting on repetition rather than regular shifts in style or medium. But these are simplifications. Again, to the casual viewer, self-taught artists — a term of convenience — can seem neither technologically inclined nor invested in "breakthroughs."

Ellen

This kind of art was about people who did not have a voice, who were not being seen by the "high" art world, yet were obsessive in making art. They were distinct individuals who also worked in similar or compatible ways. I was fascinated by the work and the common interests. The spiritual continuity among them — it blew my mind. I'm not one to explain details the way Richard does. But I knew instantly that it was what we should pursue together, to help these artists to be recognized. I knew in fact that one day they would get their place in the sun.

And again, the work fascinated me. We made a room here for it, and put in a table, and called it the "Outsider Café" (fig. 3). We had parties there and everyone would sit and talk. The very same room where that art lives today!

May I suggest a historical backdrop to your fascination? You were living together in Berkeley from 1966 to 1972, while Richard was teaching at the University of California. The Free Speech Movement and the Vietnam Day Committee had been formed the year before you arrived, setting the tone for campus activism. Haight-Ashbury, a neighborhood in nearby San Francisco, gained international notoriety during the 1967 Summer of Love. Do you see connections to the art and artists you would seek out not so many years later?

Richard

Absolutely. And there is an intellectual bridge as well. I did my PhD thesis on the economics of science and technology. In these same years, in fact, the University of Chicago published an article of mine related to inventive activity. In my studies on the subject, I learned that a lot of major inventions come from nonprofessionals. Everything from the Xerox machine — invented in the back of a beauty parlor in Astoria, Queens — to the Sidewinder missile came from nonprofessionals.[4] Outsider art appealed intellectually from this vantage. This kind of art formed an exact analogy to my field of research.

The 1960s also stands out for its popularization of deep suspicions regarding state institutions and consumerist mechanisms of control — The Establishment — as well as cries for individual and citizen liberty, summed up in the slogan "All Power to the People!"

Ellen
I helped start the Berkeley chapter of NOW, the National Organization of Women. I was tear-gassed in People's Park while nursing my first child.[5] And by the way, I had both our children at home, with natural childbirth. I also took courses at Berkeley, for example in metalsmithing. As a student there I helped to close the Berkeley Museum [*both laugh*] because they showed E. J. Bellocq images, the "women of the night," without showing the pimps or clients.[6]

I'll interject here that, while nearly everyone who knows Bellocq's highly original pictures from Belle Epoque New Orleans has seen only Lee Friedlander's prints, made in 1967–70 using Bellocq's negatives, you have here an earlier print (fig. 4)! A true rarity, in exquisite condition.

Ellen
In other words, I was an activist.

Richard
I called her, with love, Ellen the Red Menace.

Ellen
I just remembered that before the outsider artists, in fact, we had been collecting prison art! Art by incarcerated people.

Richard
Jack Kamerman, who was in the international dorm with me at University of Minnesota [1962–66], had oriented me to the importance of working with people in prison. It's not irrelevant that at the international dorm I got to know Shehu Musa from Nigeria, Sanjib Mukherjee from Kolkata and others — including a number of people from Brooklyn, who were ironically considered a part of the "international" contingent.

Ellen
And in 1963, when we got married, we saw a work by someone in prison —

Richard
— he had done a rendition of Boo Radley's house, from *To Kill a Mockingbird* —

Ellen
— I see now, this is how we started down this path!

Richard
We collected the vast amount of our outsider collection in the late seventies, early eighties.

Carl Hammer opened a gallery in Chicago in 1979, which specialized in this area, and he went on to do shows with Lee Godie, Mr. Imagination, and the estates of Jesse Howard, Bill Traylor, Eugene Von Bruenchenhein, and others.

Richard
Indeed. Jim Zanzi brought us to Carl and we became one of his first customers.

Ellen
Lisa Stone also found pieces for us, especially in photography. The point for us was the juxtaposition of the high art with work by these incredible makers. She also brought us a masterpiece by Henry Darger —

Richard
But the content was too much for me.

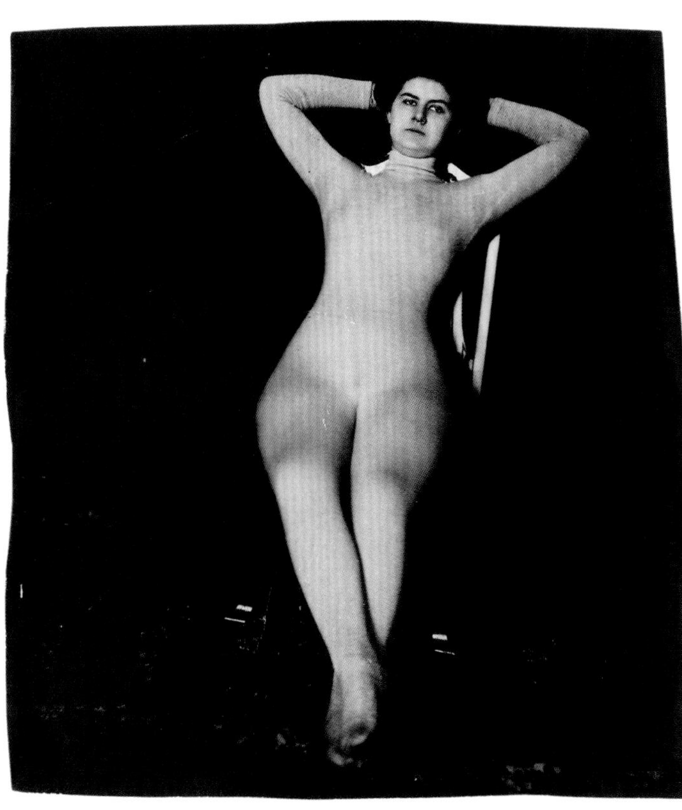

Figure 4 E. J. Bellocq (born New Orleans, 1873; died New Orleans, 1949), *Storyville Portrait*, c. 1912. Gelatin silver print; 13.6 × 11.7 cm (5 3/8 × 4 5/8 in.). Collection of Richard and Ellen Sandor.

Ellen
We had two little girls.

Richard
I tend to fall in love with the pieces I buy, and I didn't want to fall in love with this work.

Has the pace of collecting slowed at any point since then?

Figure 5 The Sandor family apartment.

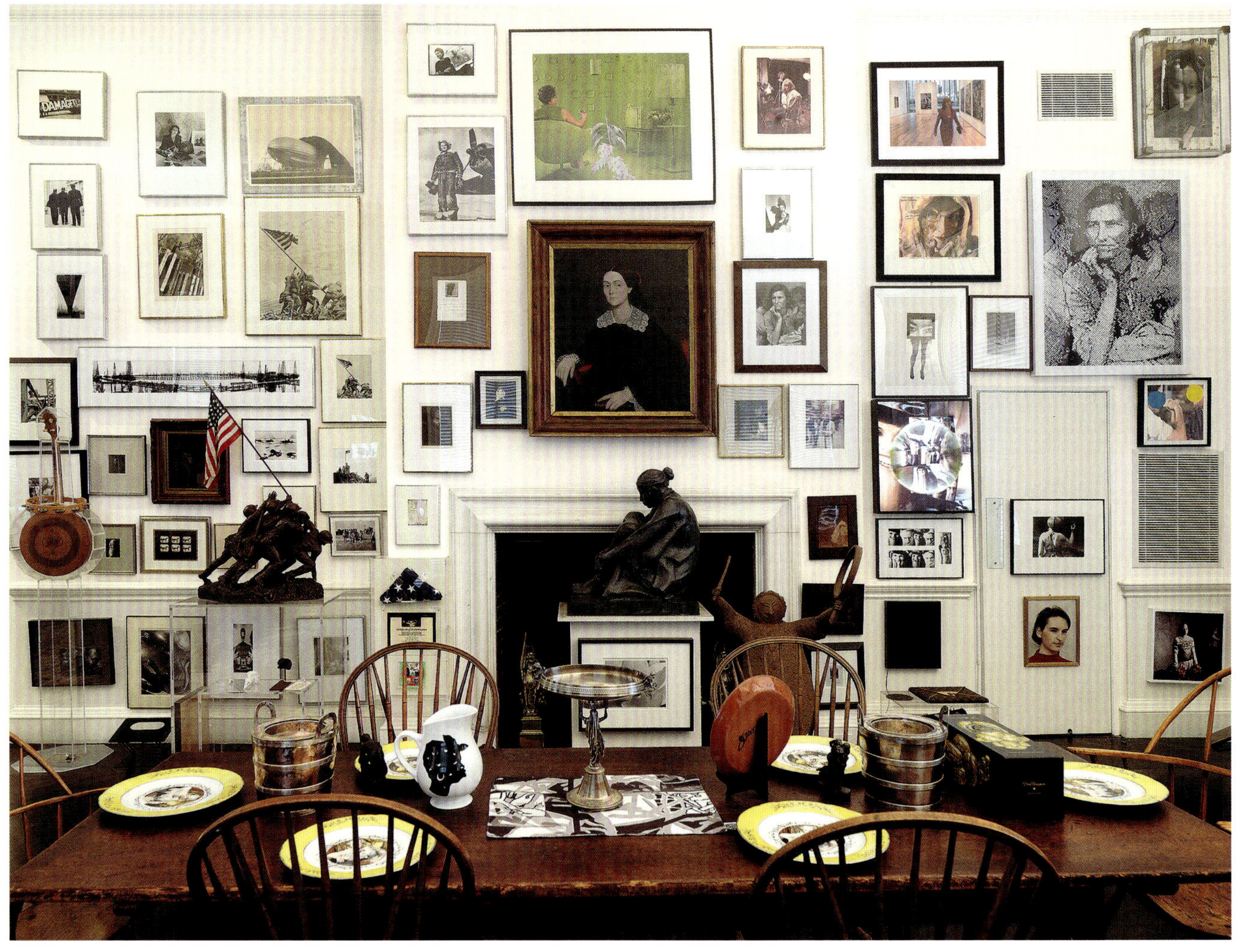

Richard
It just shifts. I'll tell you how we got pulled more heavily into photography: photography auctions, which had begun not so long before, in the early 1970s.[7] I started attending the auctions from 1980 to 1981, and there were not many people in the room — all dealers. Working on the floor of the Chicago Board of Trade, it was a comfortable space for me. And the big houses had premiums only on the seller at that time. There were very few collectors. It was a fabulous opportunity, and I was moved to bid significantly above the high estimate to get what I wanted. So the notion got out that a crazy couple in Chicago is overpaying for photographs. That brought dealers to Chicago. I'd be on the trading floor. They'd call me, lay out the photographs, I'd look and decide what I wanted in ten minutes. And then at night I would stay up looking through exhibition catalogues and other books.

Ellen
Richard would always ask me if a purchase was OK. I never said no to him.

Richard
The argument from my point of view was that I could understand the entire history of photography and bring it into our lives (see fig. 5). Czech modern, Bauhaus, nineteenth-century English, all of it. You could get your arms around it.

You see self-taught art as practiced by individuals, and the larger history that they share or advance as operating at a preconscious, spiritual level. You understand photography by contrast as a consciously unified field of technical invention whose history, as you say, can be grasped in its entirety — and in the early days of the market, possessed as well — at least through its most significant periods and protagonists. You've accordingly striven to amass examples by every major figure in photography, whereas you were never looking to own or support the work of every outlier artist. You've also worked to bring "marginal" and "major" into dialogue — to set all art on an equal footing — by valuing personal innovation above all. In your world, everyone is a modern artist.

Let's focus now on two makers who occupy multiple positions in the collection: Cindy Sherman and Kara Walker. These are artists whose work you have bought early and again more recently, and who figure prominently in your collection as they do in our time. Sherman's 1975 self-portrait as Lucille Ball (pl. 24), which she reprinted in 2001 and, I should note, inscribed to you, "To Ellen + Richard / XXOO Cindy (Lucy)," connects as you see it with the outsider works. The same goes for Walker's multipart piece Free, Black, and Passive Aggressive *(pl. 34). You also have a major light box silhouette work by Walker, which I think it's fair to interpret, in the context of the photo salon that surrounds it, as evoking precursor or early photographic technologies. Meanwhile, you presciently hailed Sherman as "ending" the history of photography — amazingly, at the very moment, in about 1980, when you were just starting to pursue that history! How did you come to your assessment?*[8]

Ellen

Hudson was my gallerist at the time and continued to be when he moved to New York. He ran Feature Inc. and brought me to those artists' work. He was such an innovator that he showed my PHSColograms (see frontispiece) with scientific and mathematical content before anyone else in Chicago or New York. Around the same time Hudson showed me basketballs floating in a tank, from the *Total Equilibrium Tanks* (1985) by Jeff Koons; unfortunately, Richard was traveling abroad and someone else got it before us. So we missed it. After that we didn't miss much.

Hudson also introduced us to the artists themselves. And Richard came up with the idea to interview the artists as to why they had made the works. We built up a trove of stories over the years (see fig. 6).

It's about wanting to embrace the future, and the new, in a way that centers the people who make the art. You want to get their stories.

Ellen

And there's another element: celebrity! CELEBRITY. For example, I saw in Hudson that he could tell who the superstars were going to be, without necessarily wanting to be a superstar himself. And at the same time Richard and I believed in speaking truth to power. He could tell in the beginning who would take off — and I could "smell" that promise too.

Richard

And back to the amount of space we have in this apartment. For example, Annette Messager (pl. 21) or Kara Walker, those works are sizable and we could fit them here (see fig. 7).

Ellen

We wanted to collect works by women, and by women of color. Richard and I both also want to get in early, knowing artists before they become superstars.

Richard

Brent Sikkema, from whom we bought the Kara Walker work, had been a photography dealer before his involvement in African American art and other directions.

Tell me about working with Gregory Warmack, a.k.a. Mr. Imagination.

Ellen

He was wonderful. He would show us, analog, everything that he wanted included in our digital pieces. We made several 3D PHSColograms with him. He insisted on adding bottle caps all around the frames of those pieces.

He was the only one whom you could meet, of the many outlier artists you collected, as he was still alive at the time. No doubt you would have loved to meet the others.

Richard
Absolutely.

Collecting shifts and changes, and these artists are not at the center of the collection now.

Ellen
Who's at the center now? Recent acquisitions include Renoir, Utrillo, early works by Rodin and Calder. Some of this reflects our interest in circus-related art since I joined the Board of the Ringling Museum of Art. We're also beginning to give our collection away!

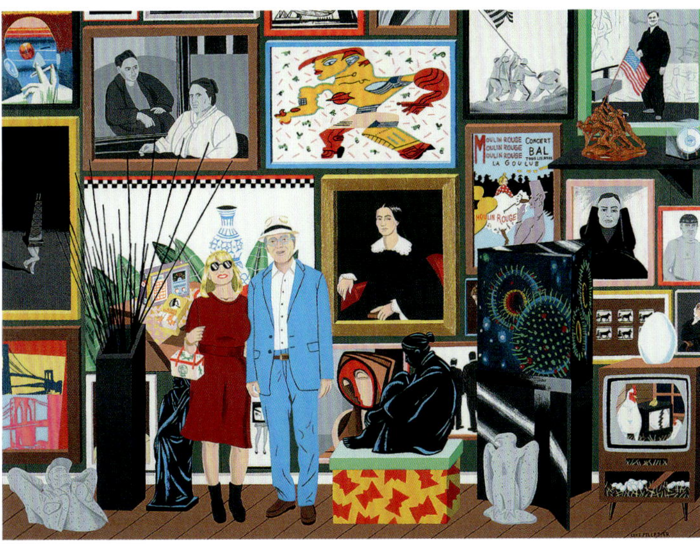

Figure 6 Luke Pelletier (born Tampa, FL, 1993; active Los Angeles). *An Opportunity to Be in a Room with the Greats, Executed in Earnest*, 2022. Acrylic on wood; 76.2 × 101.6 cm (30 × 40 in.). Collection of Richard and Ellen Sandor.

I share your conviction that all forms of art making hold equal and equivalent creative potential. As we know, moreover, photography was long considered outside the precinct of "true" or "fine" art. This "outsider" status ironically made it easier for photographers, and artists excited by photographs, to act as insurgents with respect to Fine Art. Camera images, historically at least, have given a ready means for subverting institutional hierarchies in art and questioning the wider societal presumptions that frame and maintain such hierarchies.

Richard
Exactly. Remember, when we started collecting there were maybe three museums who had photo departments: the Met, the Modern [Museum of Modern Art], and the Art Institute. Someone I admired asked me early on, "Why don't you collect real art? Photography is mechanical, etc." To which I replied, the only art form produced with no mechanical assistance is poetry! Everything else, if you take that view, is "caca."

We can see clearly from the works on your walls and in these pages that you've proven the viewpoint wrong. But many people hesitate to credit the new or revalue the underappreciated. Partly it's that they lack patience and

Figure 7 The Sandor family apartment.

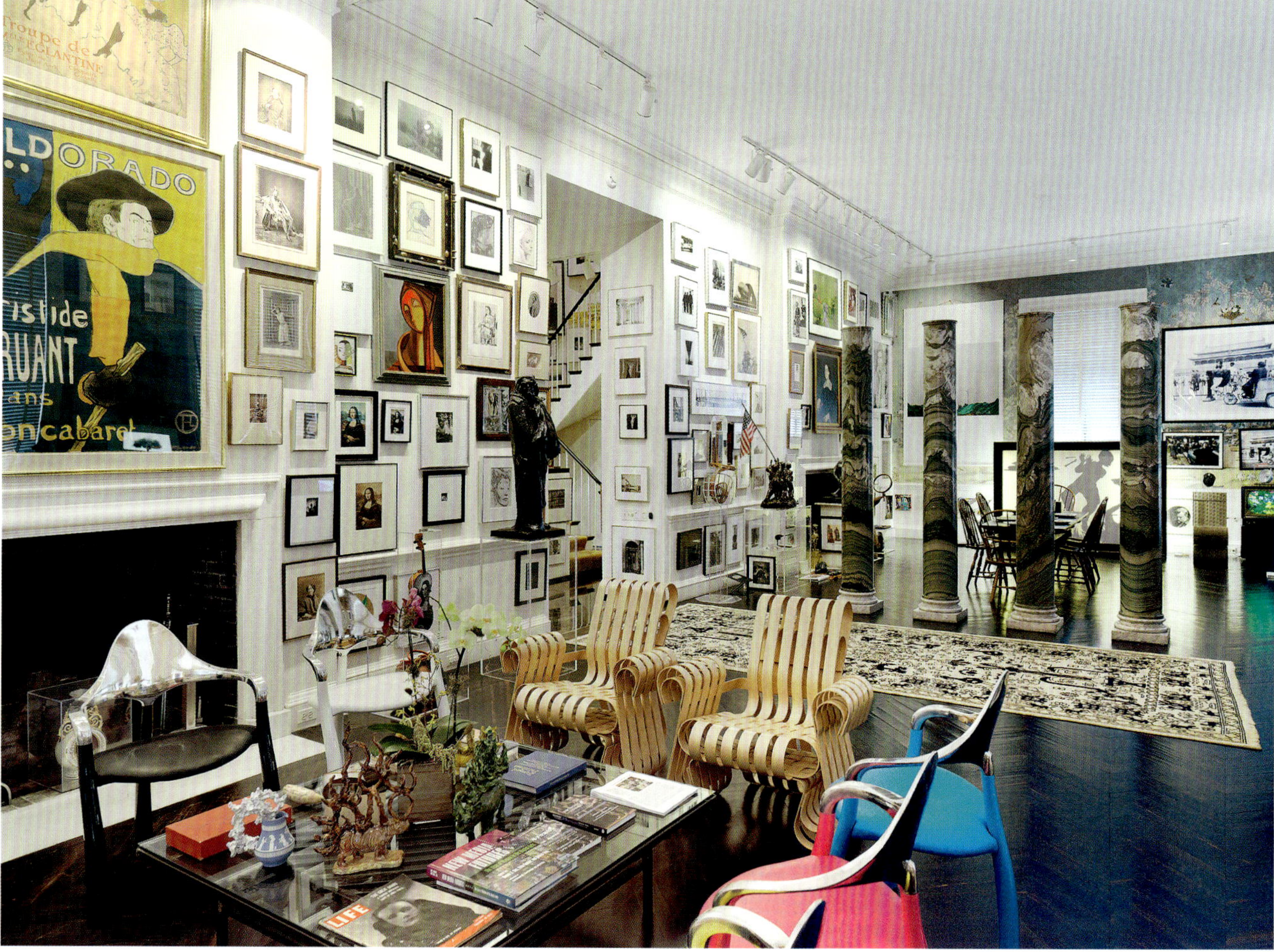

don't see revaluation happening quickly enough. As you said in one interview, Richard, a market takes a generation to fully develop; it's far slower than commonly assumed. In that interview you also said that you are attracted to environments, such as California in the 1960s and early 1970s, that don't have the baggage of historical expectations: markets for innovation "without legacy problems," as you put it.[9] *In summary, you're both comfortable with "self-made" situations and patient in assessing their development.*

Richard
Yes. At the same time, I also believe in flashes of inspiration, and Ellen does very much as well. So, I'll always wait for the next epiphany — for example for Ellen to discover an AI work that fits the collection.

Ellen
And then it will be up to museums to preserve it!

Artists and Artworks

Eddie Arning

Born Germania, TX, 1898; died McGregor, TX, 1993

The "self-made" person connotes a solitary agent, someone who acts alone. Eddie Arning does seem to have spent much of his life in relative seclusion; raised on a farm in east Texas, then estranged from his family, he spent decades in state institutional care, classed for much of that time as "mentally afflicted." Yet in his sixties and seventies, over about a decade, Arning remade himself as a practicing artist with sales and exhibitions to match. Although he preferred to work undisturbed and kept up a daily habit of long, unaccompanied walks, this great shift in identity did not happen in isolation. On the contrary, Arning's reinvention came about through conversations with a handful of well-wishers and, for a few years at the peak of his output, via a dialogue with the modern media world.

Helen Mayfield, a dancer and occupational therapist, introduced Arning to drawing in the summer of 1964.[1] For two years thereafter Arning exclusively drew scenes from his childhood and early adulthood as the son of German immigrants. When Mayfield and her husband left to spend a year in Philadelphia, Arning suddenly took up magazine illustrations as source material, leading to works such as the one shown here. By that time he had befriended Alexander Sackton, a professor of English literature at the University of Texas in Austin. Sackton became his ardent supporter, supplying Arning with his preferred crayons and drawing paper, arranging for exhibitions, and establishing a bank account in Arning's name to hold sales proceeds. Not least, Sackton used some of those proceeds to have Arning relocated from a state-run facility to the privately owned Villa Siesta, where he would have sufficient privacy and quality of care to allow his output to flourish. Sackton, the Mayfields (after their return to Texas), and a third couple, the Cogswells, formed a tight circle with Arning, who discussed his work with these friends on a near-daily basis.

In 1967, after this move, Arning worked steadily, making four to six drawings each week, which Sackton fervently catalogued. Sackton did not initially approve of Arning's shift to using magazine source imagery, fretting about "influence" on what he undoubtedly construed as Arning's unadulterated creative essence—a self that would be immanent, and therefore supposedly summoned forth rather than made. Many champions of what have been called "outsider," "self-taught," "visionary," or "intuitive" artists have cherished such fantasies of purity. Sackton soon learned to embrace Arning's approach after speaking with artist and fellow faculty

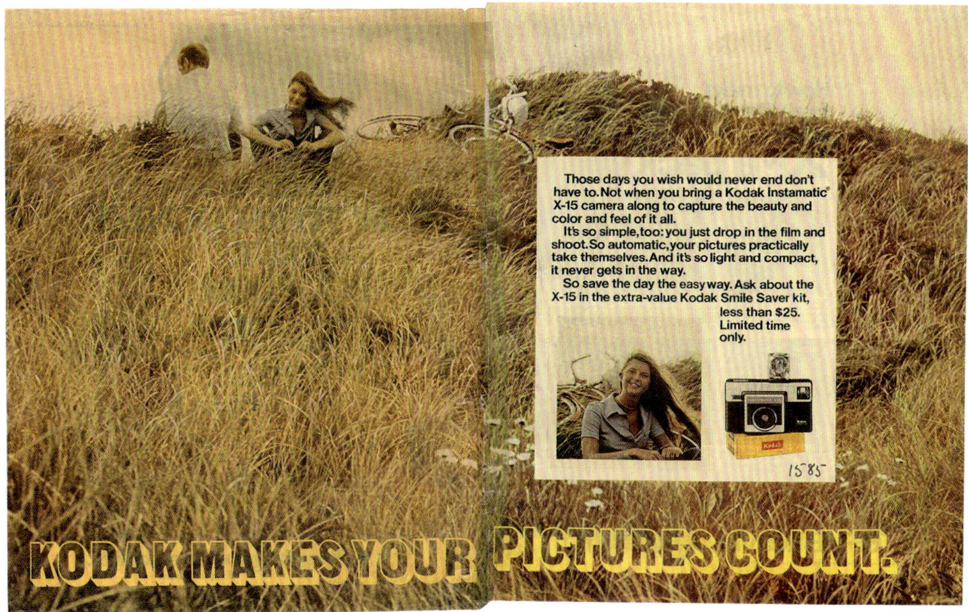

Figure 1 *Kodak Makes Your Pictures Count*, 1970–73. Published by Eastman Kodak Company (founded Rochester, NY, c. 1888). Printed matter; 33.5 × 53 cm (13 ¼ × 20 ⅞ in.). The Art Institute of Chicago, gift of Richard and Ellen Sandor, 2025.997.2.

member Kelly Fearing, although he does not seem to have let go of the notion of an unalloyed creative essence as Arning's creative wellspring: "[Fearing] suggested that the magazine illustrations were for [Arning] a form of experience from which his own picture only *began* to take shape. He has now been using pictures from magazines for *over a year* and it has not interfered with his own original ideas but only stimulated them."[2]

Scholar Pamela Jane Sachant, author of a dissertation on Arning, nevertheless observed that even after turning from childhood memories to mass-market imagery, Arning continued to gravitate toward scenes of family life and social interactions similar to those in which he found himself.[3] Sachant noted numerous instances across what we could call Arning's "magazine years" in which the artist selectively deleted or adjusted elements from the advertisements or illustrations that caught his fancy. The creative self that he was fashioning rhymed with his immediate world. Even the hilltop amid open fields in *Kodak Makes Your Pictures Count* (pl. 1)—as well as its source advertisement (fig. 1)—bears a resemblance to the topography of Villa Siesta.

In the Kodak ad drawing, Arning stands the pair of bicycles on their heads, changes the Andrew Wyeth–like sward of wheat (see fig. 2) to green, and even removes the product for sale—an Instamatic pocket camera. As personal memories were his point of initiation into drawing and provided ongoing inspiration, Arning evidently had no need of a camera or a photograph to conjure his scenes and subjects.

At least in the case of the works illustrated here, one can hazard the interpretation that dialogue is at once Arning's motivation and his subject. There is, first, an exchange between drawing and photograph, as suggested by the artist's selective omissions and reworkings. The advertisement itself sets past and present tenses in dialogue, for example, through the use of an inset that contrasts the general scene with a text and a close-up view. Foremost, however, is Arning's decision to center dialogue in his restructured image. The man and woman are not only larger and closer in his drawing than in the advertisement, but are also engaged in animated conversation, facing each other and the viewer at once as if in an Egyptian tomb painting. Having upended

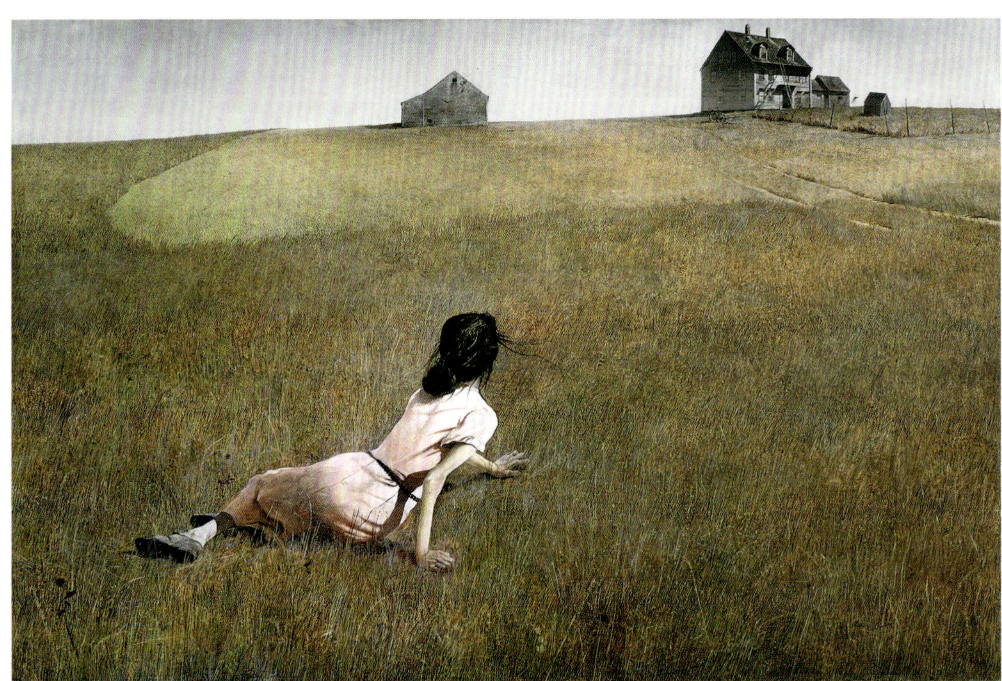

Figure 2 Andrew Wyeth (born Chadds Ford, PA, 1917; died Chadds Ford, 2009). *Christina's World*, 1948. Tempera on panel; 81.9 × 121.3 cm (32¼ × 47¾ in.). Museum of Modern Art, New York, purchase, 16.1949.

their conveyances and taken their places on the grass, they appear to be excitedly exchanging viewpoints.

Kodak would have us believe that photography facilitates connectedness, but Arning's reconfigured composition promotes dialogue and joyous memories far more straightforwardly than his source material. Still, it is enlightening to have advertisement and drawing side by side. If the advertisement promotes snapshot camera images as "self-making," either instantaneous or innocent, the drawing suggests such photographs as the fruit of sustained human exchanges.

In August 1973 the administration of Villa Siesta charged Arning with antisocial behavior and asked him to leave. Arning moved in with his sister Ida Buck, with whom he had fortuitously reconnected. The relocation cost him his circle of friends, as he was now too far for them to make more than occasional visits. Within one year Arning ceased drawing and turned to making furniture with wood he collected during his walks. Finally, nearing eighty, Arning stopped all creative work, leaving behind approximately two thousand drawings that, through the agency of Sackton and others, have landed in museum collections throughout the United States.[4]

1
Kodak Makes Your Pictures Count
1970–73
Oil pastel on paper
50.5 × 65.2 cm (19 15/16 × 25 11/16 in.)
The Art Institute of Chicago, gift of Richard and Ellen Sandor, 2025.997.1

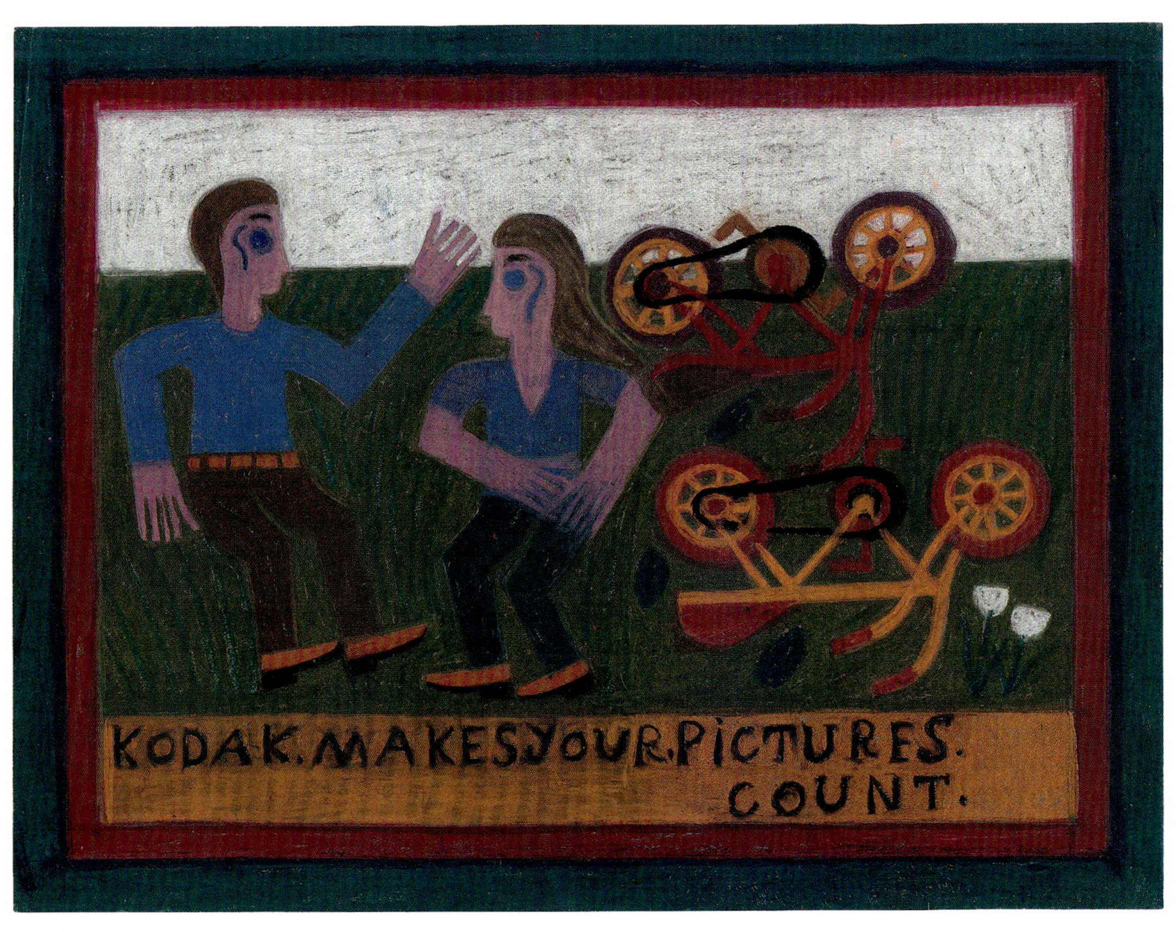

2
Untitled (Two Figures with Dog)
c. 1972
Crayon and oil pastel on paper
55.9 × 81.3 cm (22 × 32 in.)
Collection of Richard and Ellen Sandor

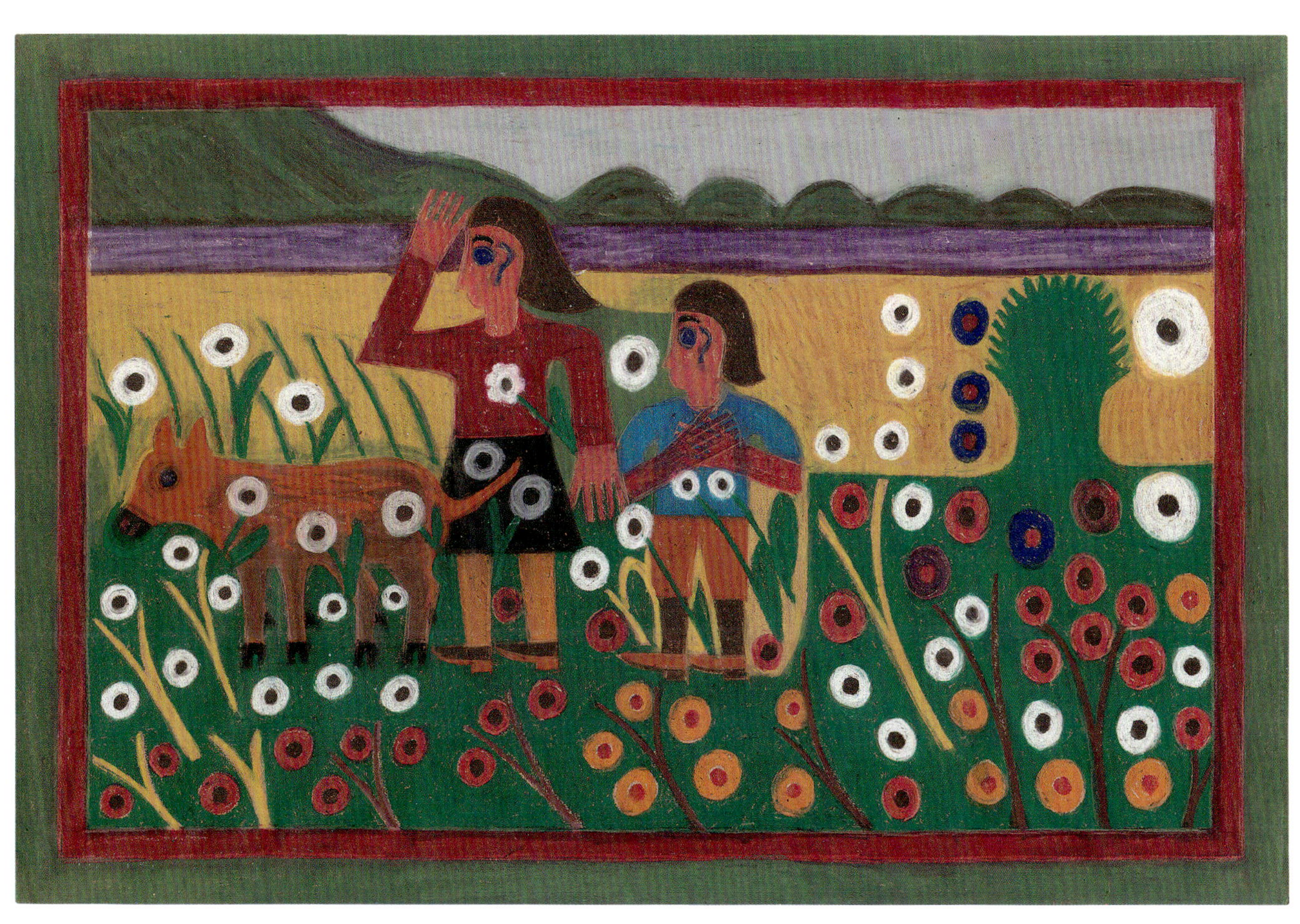

William Edmondson

Born Davidson County, TN, 1874; died Nashville, 1951

William Edmondson, like most of the "self-taught" makers in this book, redefined himself as a creative artist in middle age. Edmondson was nearly sixty when he took up stone carving, in 1931, directly upon retiring from hospital work in his hometown of Nashville; as a young man he had worked for a major railroad company in the city.[1] Initially carving headstones for local Black cemeteries, Greenwood West (formerly Mount Ararat) and Greenwood, Edmondson filled his front yard with sculptures of animals, angels, and figures of importance in Black America, such as boxer Jack Johnson and First Lady Eleanor Roosevelt. In 1937 Edmondson enjoyed a solo exhibition of his work at the Museum of Modern Art (MoMA) in New York, which had been founded just two years before he took up carving. As art historian Robert Farris Thompson wrote, Edmondson "was spiritually ambitious but down to earth" and never let the honor of being the first person of African descent to have a one-person show at MoMA go to his head.[2]

Edmondson turned to art at a propitious time, as MoMA and other cultural institutions, alongside agencies of the United States government, all upheld "folk art" as a nationally significant creative domain throughout the 1930s. Louise Dahl-Wolfe, a photographer for fashion magazines including *Harper's Bazaar*, was operating in this current when she made a suite of portraits of Edmondson in 1936, as well as images of the sculptor at work—photographs that led directly to the show at MoMA the following year (funded in part through the Works Progress Administration [WPA]). Edward Weston took photographs of Edmondson (see figs. 1–2) in September 1941 while crisscrossing the country on a commission to illustrate a bibliophile edition of Walt Whitman's *Leaves of Grass*, a classic of American literature first published on Independence Day in 1855.[3] Edmondson himself was hired as a sculptor by the WPA in 1939 and 1940, completing this particular circle of interest.

Figure 1 Edward Weston (born Highland Park, IL, 1886; died Carmel Highlands, CA, 1958). *William Edmondson, Sculptor*, 1941. Gelatin silver print; 19.1 × 24.1 cm (7½ × 9½ in.). The Art Institute of Chicago, gift of Richard and Ellen Sandor, 2025.889.

Figure 2 Weston. *Carvings of William Edmondson of Nashville*, 1941. Gelatin silver print; 19.1 × 24.1 cm (7½ × 9½ in.). The Art Institute of Chicago, gift of Richard and Ellen Sandor, 2025.888.

Weston's wife, writer Charis Wilson, who diarized their 1941 trip, described Edmondson's yard and his greeting in lines that match the sculpture and photographs reproduced here: "Dotted over the green turf are horses, birds, squirrels, rams, imaginary animals, women angels, rabbits, eagles. In front of the shed a pile of uncut stones—hunks of limestone from wrecked buildings. Edmondson sits under the shed roof on a flat cut stump chiseling away at a stone. He is pleased to see us and tells Edward to make all the pictures he wants."[4]

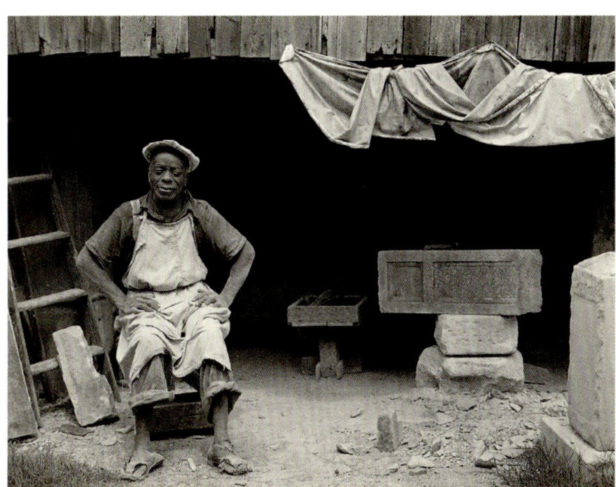

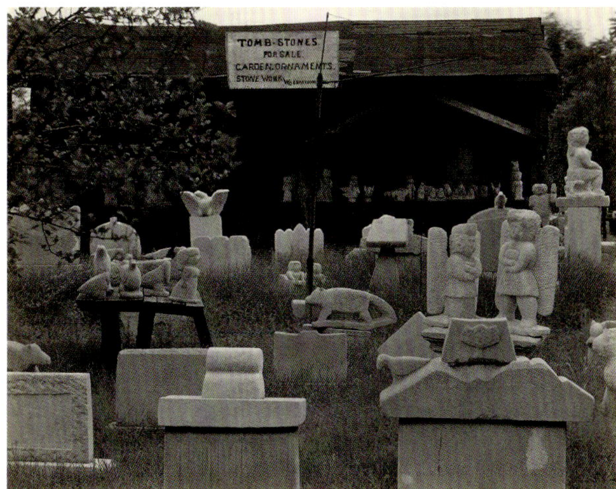

Such a welcome seems plausible and suggests Edmondson's practiced ease at receiving visitors from far beyond Black Nashville. Farris Thompson's description of Edmondson's general demeanor and his pose in this particular photograph, however, also seem plausible: "He radiates cool.... [Such] self-assertion comes through a photograph that Edward Weston took in 1941. Edmondson sits next to a ladder, in cap, clothes, and apron. He averts his head (being distant but respectful). But he [also] places hands on his thighs, with angled-out elbows. To sit, arms akimbo, is in Kongo a sign of debate or confrontation (*ntantani evo mpaka*)." Farris Thompson cited in summation a line from an interview he conducted in 1999 with Evelyn Edmondson Hill, a registered nurse in Nashville and the sculptor's grandniece: "you can take my picture, but you can't take my mind."[5]

Self-possession is central to self-making. The controlled force and precision necessary for stone carving can in Edmondson's case be understood as material translations of the strength of character needed to establish oneself in the world, particularly later in life and with a humble background.

Additionally, and crucially, Edmondson offered a parable of origins for his breakthrough into art that spoke of a higher power: "I heard a voice telling me to pick up my tools and start to work on a tombstone. I looked up in the sky and right there in the noon daylight He hung a tombstone out for me to make ... I knowed it was God telling me what to do."[6]

To be "possessed" in a spiritual way is to listen to oneself and one's community; it is to accept a calling, and is thus in fact a manifestation of great will and a drive toward freedom.

Farris Thompson interpreted the many single birds that Edmondson carved, including a number of eagles, as signs of liberation. He noted that Edmondson positioned some of these birds atop a supporting tombstone, poised for flight, and that the stones themselves were sited on the rising slope of a hill; and he cited the artist's grandniece once more: "These birds remind us we'll not always be on earth—there'll come a day when we fly away, like the 'fly away' poem of the old spiritual song." Farris Thompson also cited research which suggests that dreams of flight as or with birds appear with special intensity in African American narratives, for example Harriet Tubman recalling that her determination to flee enslavement, as well as the path she took, were heralded in a dream "in which she saw herself flying over the northern area to which she was eventually to escape to freedom."[7]

In this sense one can also interpret Edmondson's birds, or at least this particular eagle (pl. 3), as a self-portrait. It is not a bird in flight, as shown on the reverse face of the United States quarter in Edmondson's time, nor is it grasping the arrows and olive branches that stand for America's ability to wage war and peace in depictions on the US dollar bill or the insignia of the 1933 National Recovery Act.[8] This eagle spreads its wings yet stands its ground, contained, ready for flight or fight as the encounter may demand. One could even liken the position to that adopted by Edmondson in Weston's photograph: *ntantani evo mpaka*, arms akimbo. The raptor has only a patch of stone on which to perch, yet it holds its chest out and keeps its beak high. It knows what it is made of, and further, that it and the earth are composed from one and the same material. Together they are indomitable.

3
Eagle
c. 1940s
Limestone
56.6 × 39.4 × 18.5 cm
(22¼ × 15½ × 7¼ in.)
The Art Institute of Chicago, gift of Richard and Ellen Sandor, 2025.611

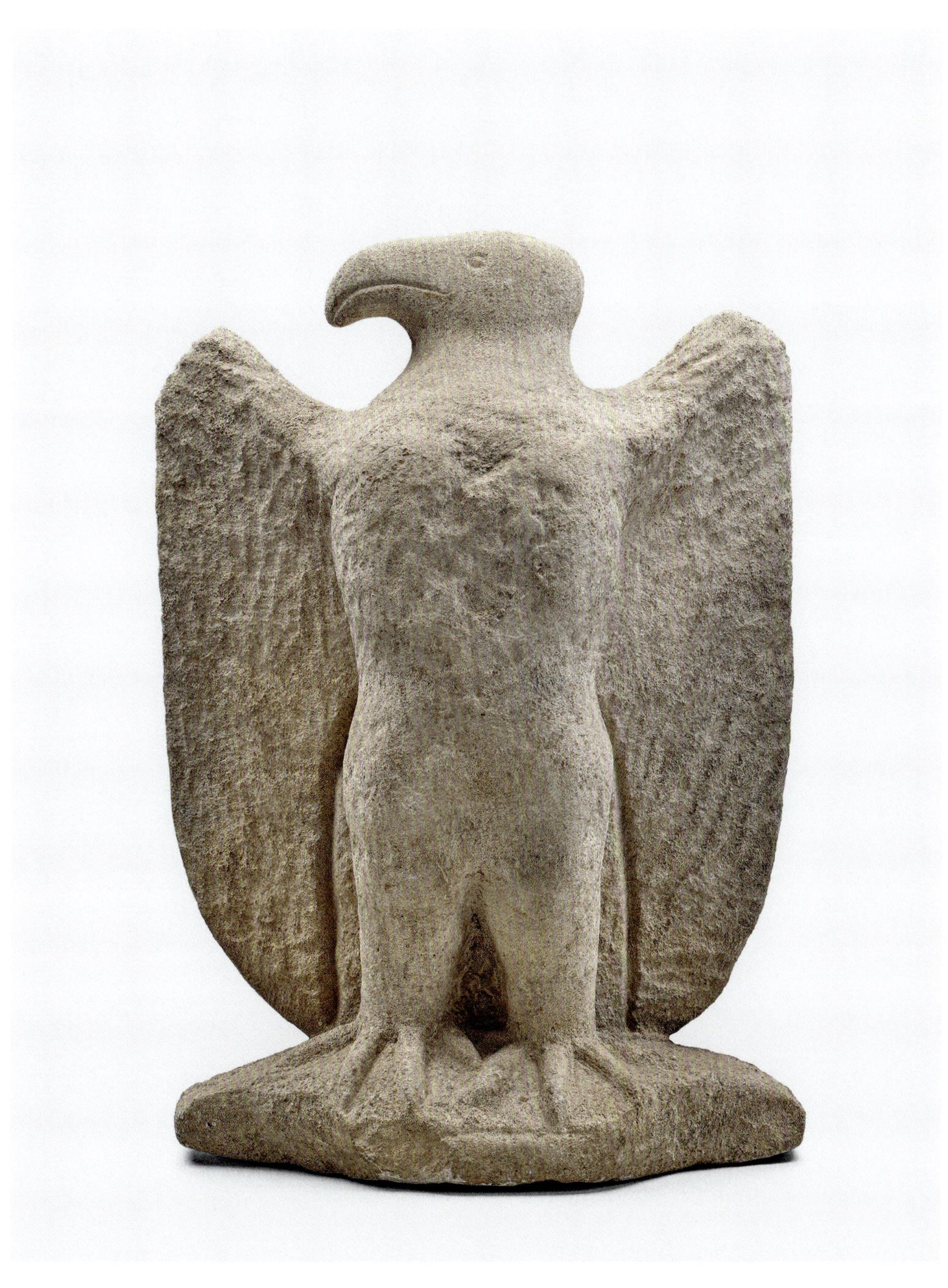

Lee Godie

Born Chicago, 1908; died Plato Center, IL, 1994

Lee Godie is among the clearest examples in this book of a constructed self, in the sense not only of reinvention but also of an ongoing, sustained focus on selfhood as the motor of her art. Born Jamot Emily Godee, she lived under one or perhaps two married names before taking her *nom d'artiste* by 1968, when she materialized on the steps of the Art Institute of Chicago to hawk her paintings and drawings. Although a great raconteur, Godie kept private many details of her biography, deepening the sense of a rift that separated "Lee Godie" from whomever she had been before. At the same time, Godie made portraits of stars and icons, and especially self-portraits *as* a star or icon. These were the mainstay of her art career and the font of inspiration for her varied and shifting post-1968 guises.

Self-fashioning accordingly constitutes a central theme in assessments of Godie, and it functions quite differently than it does in the work of artists such as Cindy Sherman (see p. 72) — even though Sherman admires and owns Godie's work. Godie literalized self-portraiture, at least initially, by applying brushwork to her own face. "She was quite striking," recalled an early patron, "because her face was all painted, which is something she very seldom did after that. She had big orange balls painted on each cheek, painted eye shadow, and eyebrows painted above her actual ones, all from the same paint box she was making her pictures with."[1] One could read Godie's doubling of her eyebrows as a move to underscore the artifice of her performance, or to comment on artifice as central to art making generally. However, as curator Valérie Rousseau has observed, "[Godie's] immersive stance and total engagement blur the frontiers between art and life ... the profound intimacy that emanates from these works arises in part from their solemn, unironic stakes."[2] Godie's artistic identity was no act or persona: it was her self.

The sincerity with which Godie inhabited her creative identity seems beyond question. Michael Bonesteel, who organized a thorough exhibition of Godie's paintings, drawings, and photographs in 1993 at the Chicago Cultural Center, detailed her eccentricities in the accompanying catalogue. These run the gamut from the practical—eating only the crispy skin of barbecued chicken legs, and not the meat, because she lacked sufficient teeth to chew—to the provocative, such as finding pants unladylike while wearing a bra on top of her clothes. Bonesteel also described the unhoused life that Godie tenaciously maintained for more than twenty years, roughly from her sixtieth birthday until after she turned eighty-two. Godie perambulated a one-and-a-half-square-mile area that stretched north from the Art Institute to the Drake Hotel, and approximately from Michigan Avenue west to Clark: making art in various parks; storing or retrieving supplies from rented lockers in department stores, bus terminals, and parking garages; overnighting on benches, clad in pieced-together rabbit-skin coats; and wearing men's orthopedic shoes for winter warmth. Godie repeatedly refused her own daughter's offers of indoor quarters until beset by arthritis and worsening Parkinson's disease. Money was not the issue, Bonesteel explained, for Godie had savings and also sold her paintings effectively: "She was always financially solvent. She *chose* to live the way she did."[3]

Testimonials, and above all the works themselves, evidence just as clearly that Godie understood art and the life of an artist as an incessant set of conversations. She elected radical self-reliance, turning her back on family and even her own past, but she made art that depended essentially on discussion or debate with others—and precisely a debate over aesthetics and creative identity, one that she initiated by issuing a challenge to the most famous artists she knew. When Godie ascended the Art Institute steps it was to proclaim herself superior to Paul Cezanne.[4] She studied the museum's French nineteenth-century collections closely, even while sparring with their stars as well as her audience: "Renoir was the greatest artist of all time. He always said he painted beauty. Now I always try to paint beauty, but some people say my paintings aren't beautiful. Well, I have beauty in my mind, but it isn't always easy to make paintings beautiful."

The archetypes that people Godie's paintings and drawings, ranging from Flaming Youth to the Gibson Girl and a Bismarck-era military figure she called The Hessian, constitute another set of conversation partners. Godie drew upon the overlapping spheres of film and fashion; Flaming Youth, for instance, appears to have been modeled on silent film star Clara Bow, and Godie repeatedly made herself up as

Joan Crawford or Katharine Hepburn. What in canonical modernist art could be read as a play on doubling, whether to question art as the production of singular objects or to cast doubt on the uniqueness of the creative ego, seems in Godie's case to be more productively understood as a paradoxical "one-way dialogue." A series of drawings from the 1980s called *Hands* (pl. 8), which involve from four to as many as ten differently colored but otherwise identical hands saluting a stretch-limo keyboard like so many Rockette legs, precisely images art as a dialogue carried out by one person alone. So does a story of Godie acquiescing at last, and with evident reluctance, to a request by a longtime supporter named David Syrek for a commissioned portrait. Syrek unrolled the canvas that Godie had hastily shoved under his arm and saw two identically shaped birds, one red and one blue: the artist and her patron.

Godie conversed from the sidelines with French painters and film stars. She also talked to and argued with herself. "Lee — I kept saying left side," reads the caption in one photograph (pl. 4), for which she bared her shoulders and collarbones (of which she was proud), as if she had to coerce herself into an artistically worthy pose. There is more than a hint of dissociative personality disorder in this caption, as in stories that recount Godie hearing voices: Renoir's ghost telling her to make money with her brushes, or a red bird instructing her to take up painting. Yet if Godie might not have acted with the ironic intent of an artist schooled in postmodern philosophy and institutional critique, this does not mean that her (self-)inventive aesthetics should be deemed unselfconscious or reduced to a sign of unstable mental health. States of mind are just as rich a source of creative insight as art and society, and Godie's work shows that all these domains can be brought into a generative exchange.

Godie was a writer as well as a visual artist; she tried to publish her poems and kept a long-running journal. An entry from one frigid winter day interweaves the form and subjects of her discursive creativity as a street artist with the concision of a line of verse by Emily Dickinson. Writing in a tone of advice tinged with self-criticism, Godie rallied her courage against the bitter cold: "Lee to Lee — When I warm my knee-caps well — then I rise up and down with simplicity."

4
Lee — I Kept Saying Left Side and Grooves till I Got to the Camera Sincerily
1970s
Gelatin silver print
12.1 × 9.6 cm (4 ¾ × 3 ¾ in.)
The Art Institute of Chicago, gift of Richard and Ellen Sandor, 2025.872

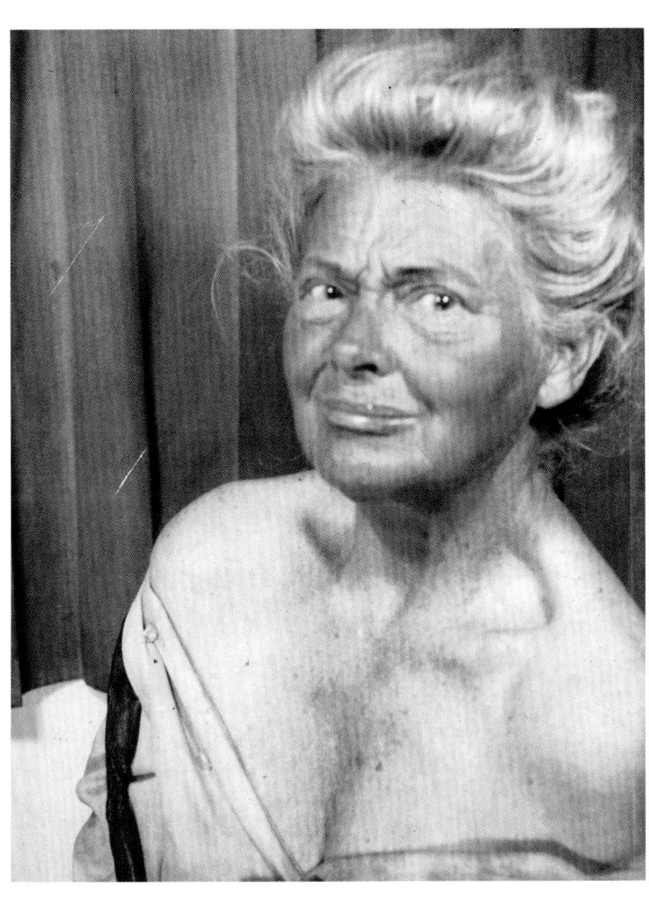

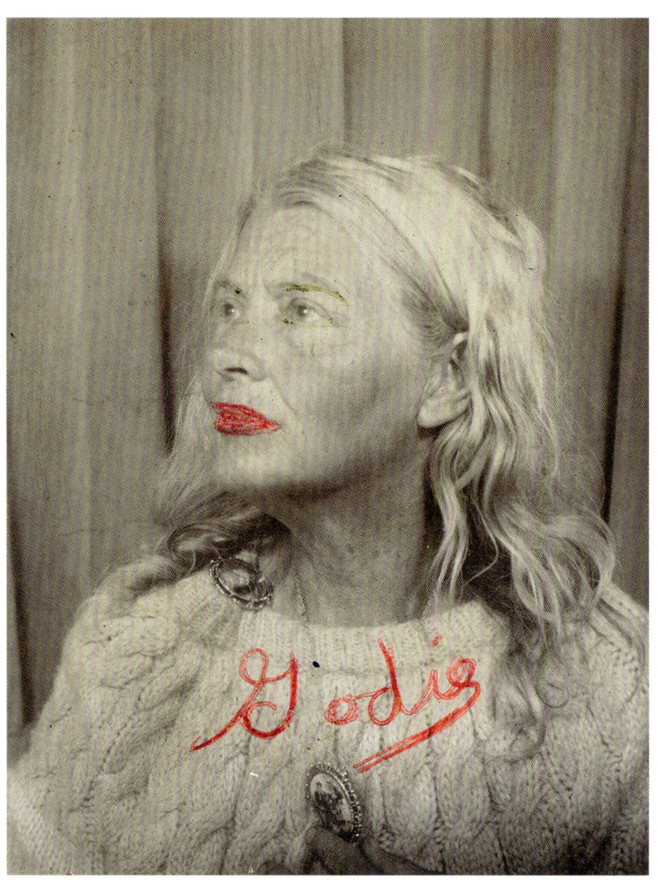

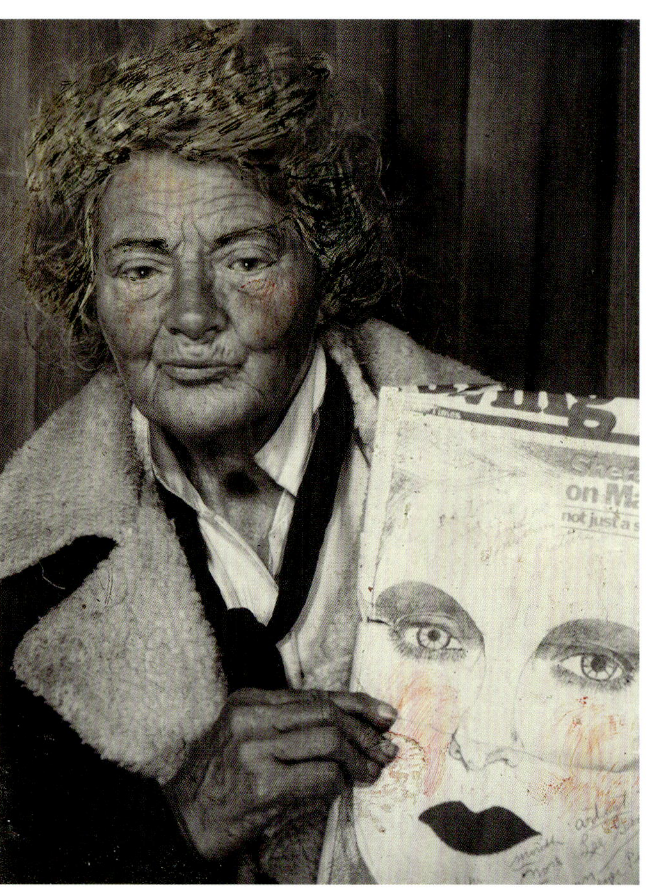

5
Lee and Cameo on a Chair Sincerily Lee Godie
1970s
Gelatin silver print with ink
12.1 × 9.6 cm (4¾ × 3¾ in.)
The Art Institute of Chicago, gift of Richard and Ellen Sandor, 2025.873

6
This Is a News Front Page Picture …
1970s
Gelatin silver print with ink
12.1 × 9.6 cm (4¾ × 3¾ in.)
The Art Institute of Chicago, gift of Richard and Ellen Sandor, 2025.874

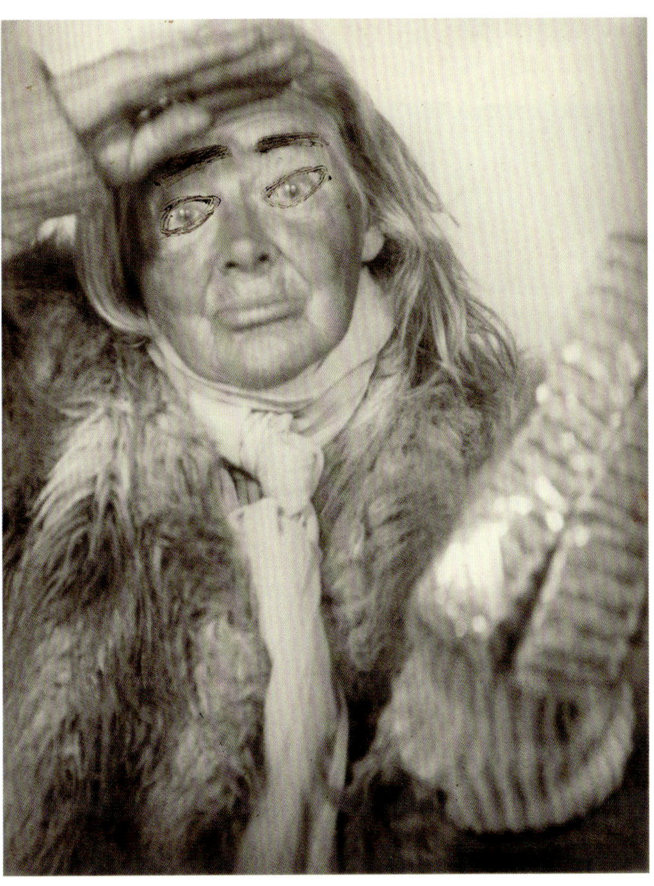

7
Lee — When My Coat Was New Sincerily
1970s
Gelatin silver print with ink
12.1 × 9.6 cm (4¾ × 3¾ in.)
The Art Institute of Chicago, gift of Richard and Ellen Sandor, 2025.875

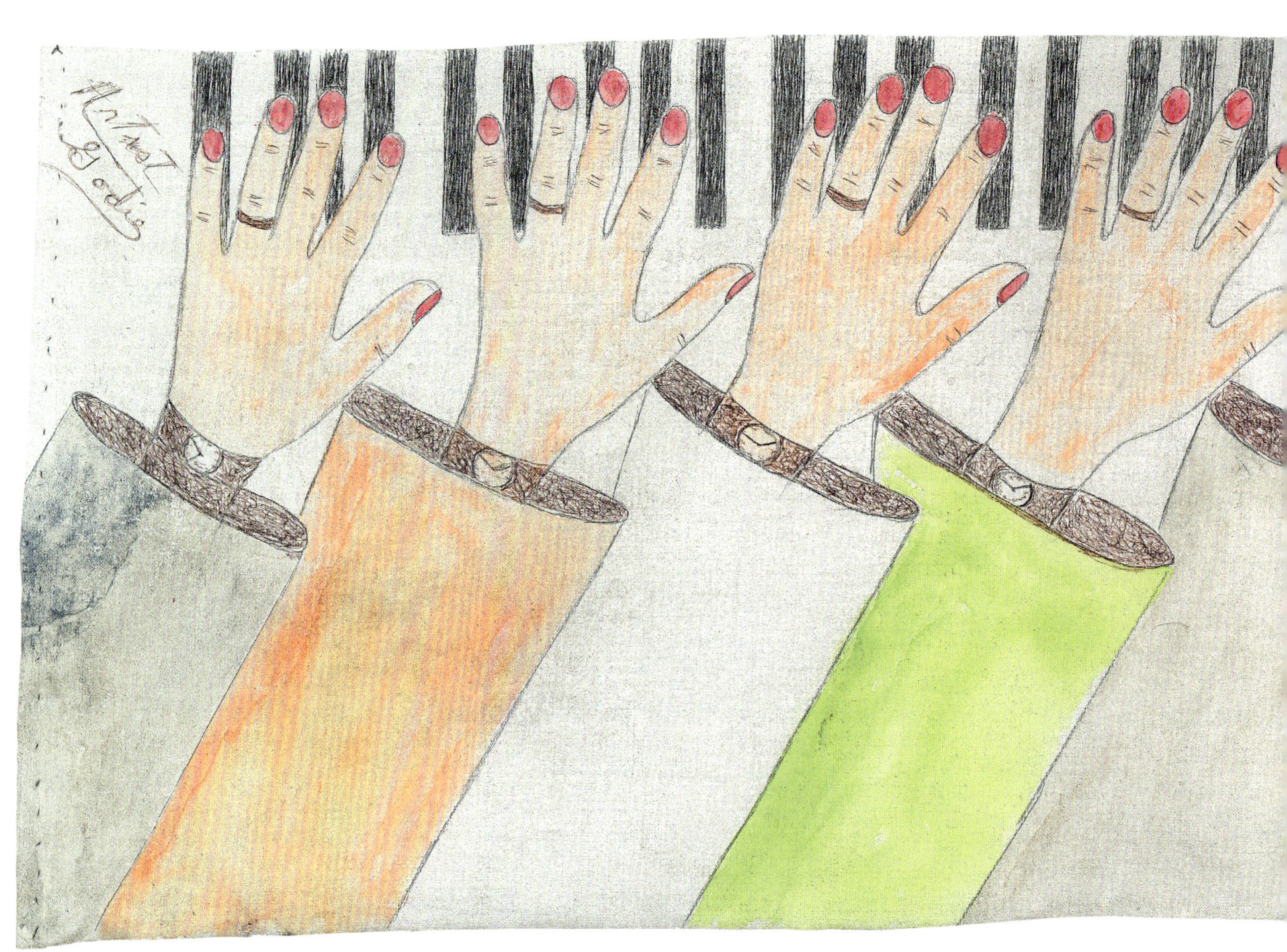

8
Hands
1980s
Watercolor, ballpoint pen, and graphite on canvas
45.5 × 129.5 cm (17 15/16 × 51 in.)
The Art Institute of Chicago, gift of Richard and Ellen Sandor, 2025.1001

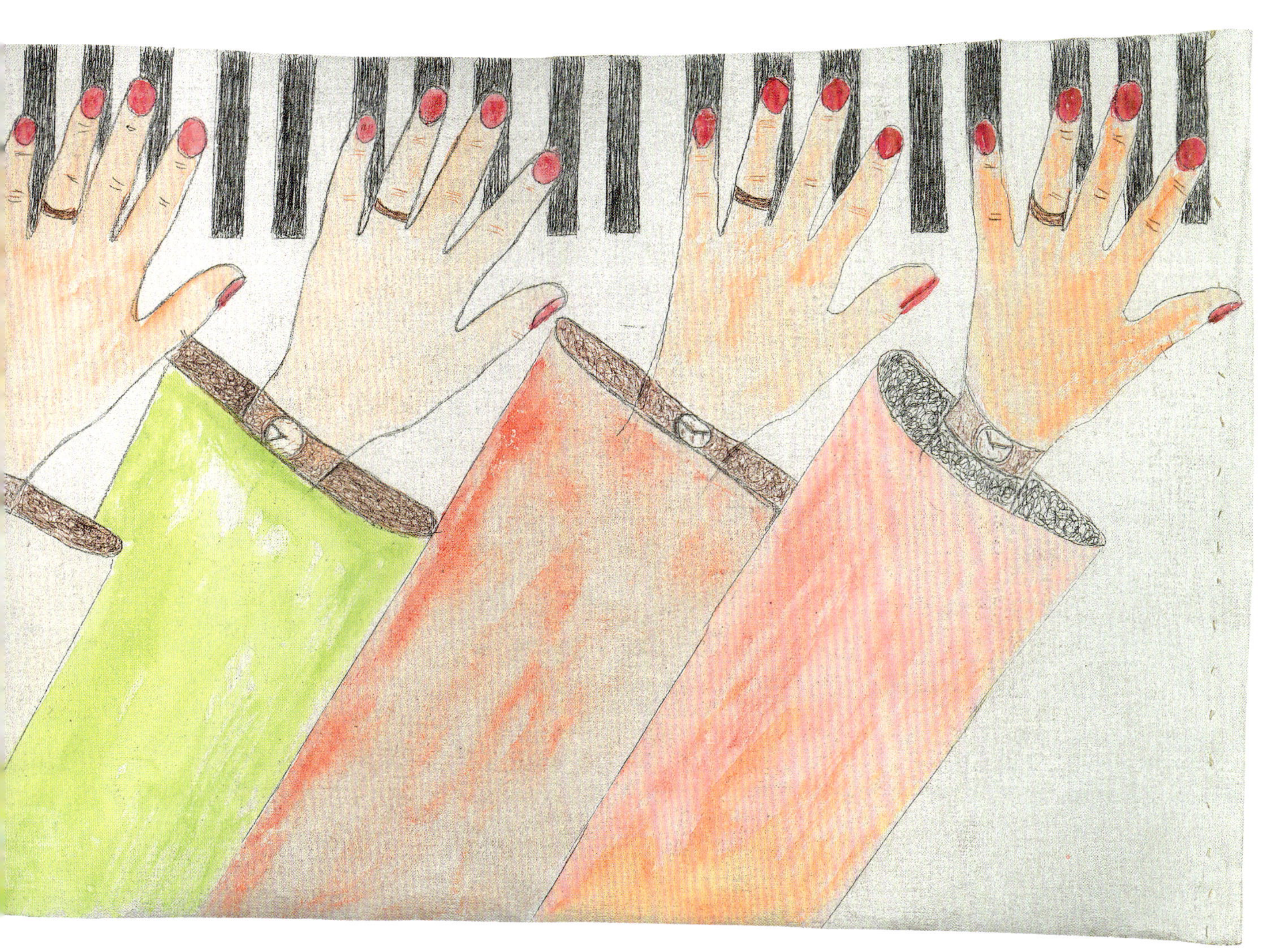

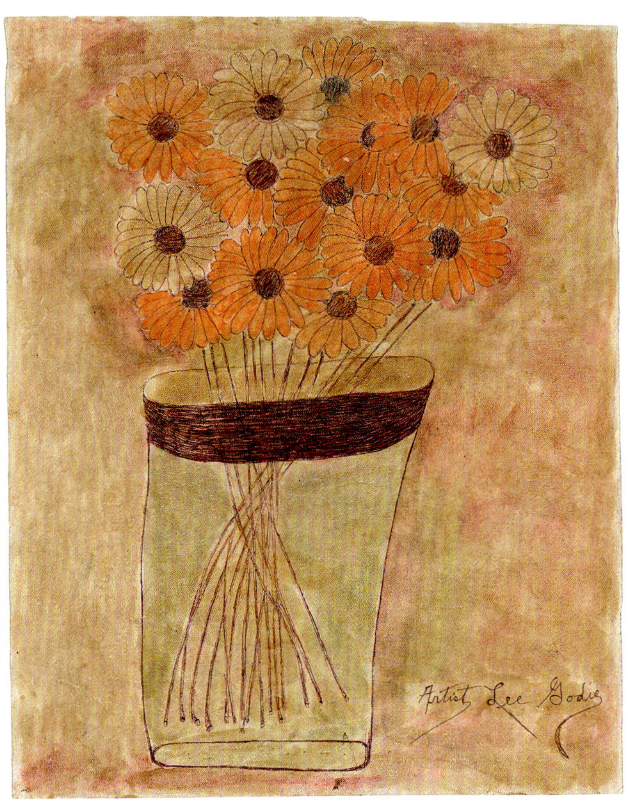

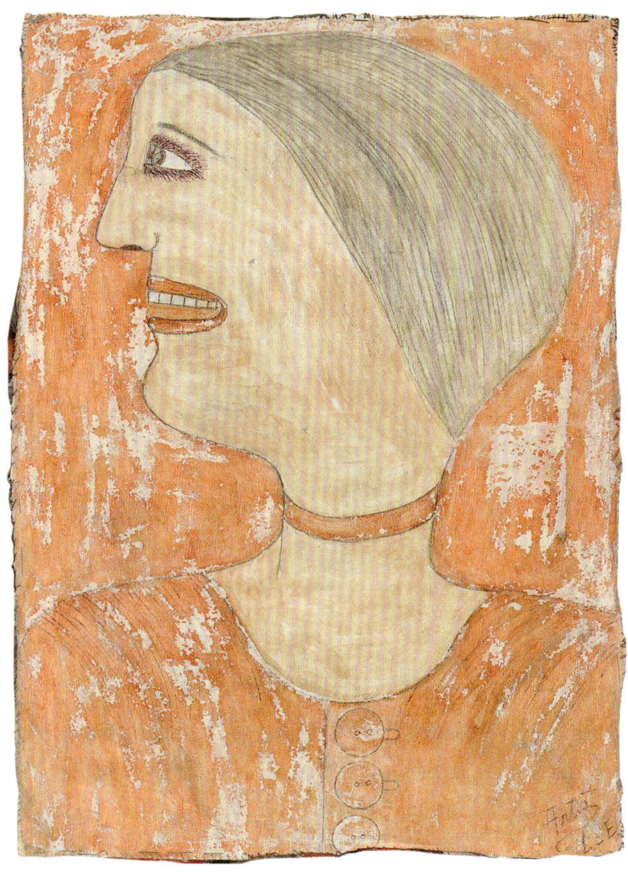

9
Daisies White and Orange
1970s–80s
Watercolor and ballpoint pen on canvas
58.4 × 46 cm (23 × $18\frac{1}{8}$ in.)
The Art Institute of Chicago, gift of Richard and Ellen Sandor, 2025.998

10
Profile Portrait
1970s–80s
Paint and ballpoint pen with graphite on canvas sewn to synthetic fabric
65.5 × 47.5 cm ($25\frac{13}{16}$ × $18\frac{3}{4}$ in.)
The Art Institute of Chicago, gift of Richard and Ellen Sandor, 2025.999

11
Be My Valentine
1970s–80s
Paint and ballpoint pen on canvas
60.7 × 91 cm (23 15⁄16 × 35 7⁄8 in.)
The Art Institute of Chicago, gift of Richard and Ellen Sandor, 2025.1000

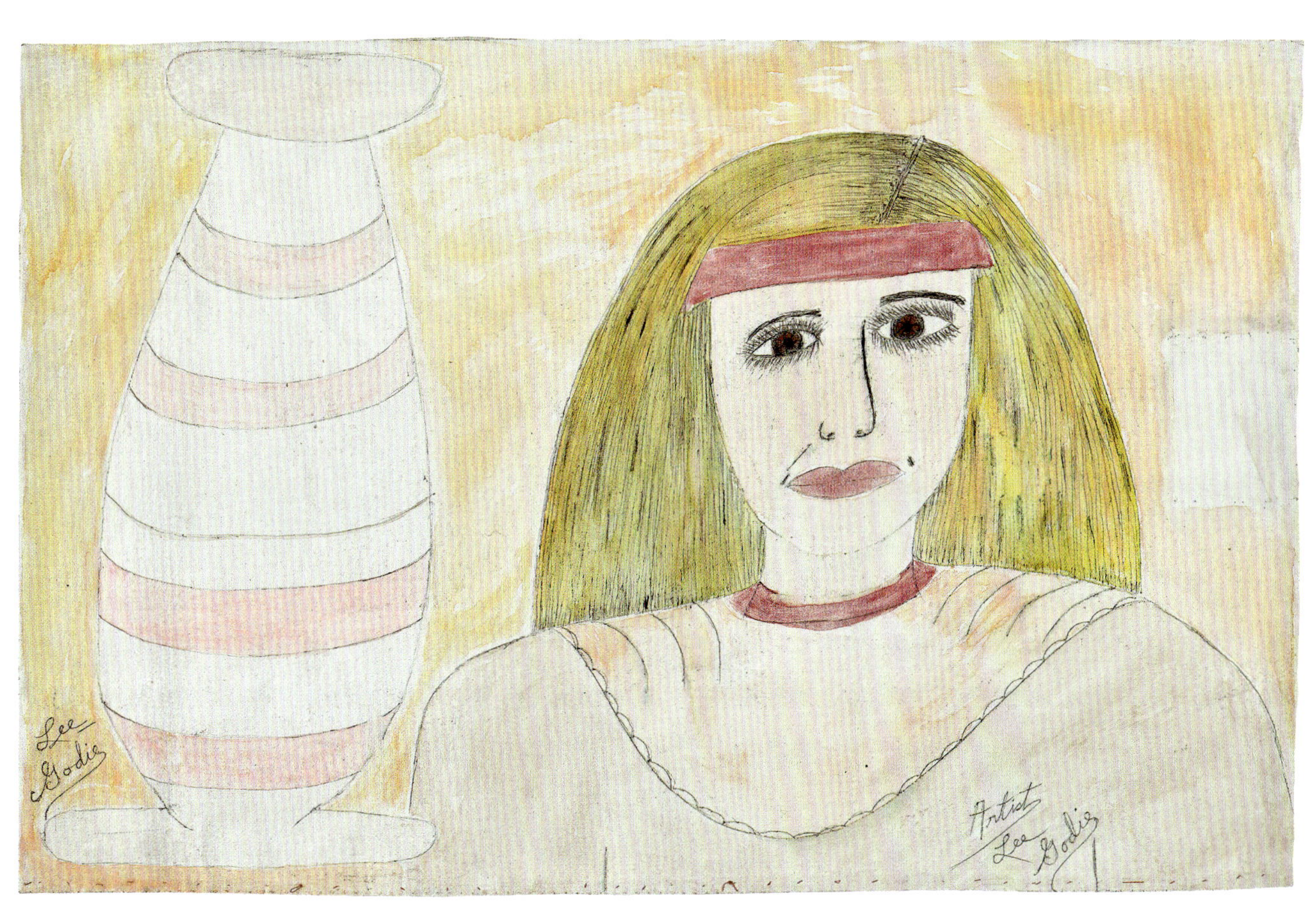

Jesse Howard

Born Shamrock Township, MO, 1885; died Fulton, MO, 1983

To speak one's mind, consistently and forcefully, can be a creative act. It can also be the work of a crank or a madman. In 1944 Jesse Howard settled in Fulton, Missouri, whose townspeople quickly opposed his views and activities, and defaced or stole some of the densely worded signs with which he populated his twenty-acre homestead.[1] Howard apparently retaliated by traveling to Washington, DC, to seek compensation through a lawsuit. He stood as steadfast as his signage and did not shy from notoriety.

The self that Howard constructed, after spending his younger years as a migrant laborer on the West Coast, was one of transparent conviction. He quoted Biblical passages and news sources in turn, with a mixture of unattributed opinions that address current events precisely in the tone and language of a hectoring preacher: "CORRUPTION. DID YOU EVER SEE A BALL OF MAGGOTS WORKING IN AN OLD DEAD CARCUS? WELL, THAT REPRESENTS THE DAMNED COMMUNIST. THEY, THE COMMUNIST ARE NO GOOD. ANY COMMENT?" (pl. 20). The final words are an empty gesture, for Howard's edge-to-edge typography and condemnatory language leave no room for debate.

Independence of thought, the hallmark of Howard's rhetoric, appears to apply to him alone; his declamations seem addressed to a world that is benighted and generally beyond hope of enlightenment. "BRAIN WASHED YESSER . . ." begins another sign (pl. 16), despairing of all received wisdom. Admonishment follows only naturally, as in his sign that relates the story of a boy killed in a car accident occasioned by uncontrolled rage ("ANGRY, AND TEMPER CAUSES BOY

TO LOOSE HIS LIFE ...") (pl. 15), or his summary review of events leading to the arrest and trial in Jerusalem of Adolf Eichmann, a principal logistician of the Nazi Holocaust, painstakingly painted on metal ("ST. LOUIS GLOBE. FRI. DEC. 30. 1960. GOETTINGEN. WEST GERMANY ... ") (pl. 14).

If Howard's creative contribution depended solely on the text of his works, it would likely be slight. Two factors combine, however, to make these exhortatory signs not only noteworthy but remarkable. One is the quality of Howard's sign-painting—assured and steady—which reinforces the preacherly stream of consciousness through his inventive use of punctuation and the all-caps, edge-to-edge lettering. The American South has a rich history of vernacular Biblical signage, as attested by Walker Evans's Depression-era photographs or literary sources such as *Wise Blood* by Flannery O'Connor, among others. Howard extended this tradition and enriched it through the diversity of his topics of interest.

Howard also made language sculptural and, more audaciously, transformed it into a public-facing built environment. The signs that came to fill his property were painted, but they were always also objects, and even structures, and that is how spectators reacted to them—whether in admiration or outrage. Gregg Blasdel, an artist who brought initial art-world attention to Howard through a 1968 magazine article on "grass-roots" makers, glossed his production as "signs that have always been stolen or blasted with buckshot from cars making that particular turn in the road"; Blasdel noted and illustrated in particular "[Howard's] roadside fence facade [erected] to display his sentiments to the public."[2] This brings Howard's project into line with the works of Simon Rodia, Fred Smith, and other makers whom Blasdel and future writers would categorize as "intuitive" creators, isolated from art history and ripe for "discovery" by the art establishment. It also makes that project at least distantly compatible with those of artists who, then or later, have taken such parasculptural communication formats as billboards, wall newspapers, and electronic signs as a platform or a model of public engagement.

In a much closer way, Howard's dedication to creating a word-environment addressed to the general public matches that of Fluxus artist Ben Vautier, who established his anti-art *magasin* or "shop" (fig. 1) in the South of France in 1958, roughly contemporaneous with Howard working in the Southern United States. Ben, as he was known, asked the world to "doubt everything" while accepting that "everything is art."[3] He defended the rights of ethnic groups and languages, in particular Occitan in his home region, against nationalism and global hegemonies. Not as exclusively logocentric as Howard, Ben nevertheless covered the indoor and outside surfaces of his makeshift storefront with hortatory aphorisms that were brightly painted in a childlike cursive on black backgrounds.

Critical consensus is long past assessing eccentric or obsessive makers as untutored or aesthetically naive. The many popular or vernacular realms of expression mined by modern and contemporary artists, and the innumerable industrial or banal materials legitimated in or as art through their practices, render moot the categorical separation of "high" and "low," "insiders" and "outliers," as a lengthening line of books and exhibitions has persuasively argued.[4] Even so, the loose resemblance and coincidence of dates between Ben's looping koans and Howard's finely lettered sermonizing can be a red herring: The artists' divergent backgrounds and aims, and the disparate contexts of production and reception for their works, demand a more thorough side-by-side examination than can be provided in a short catalogue entry.

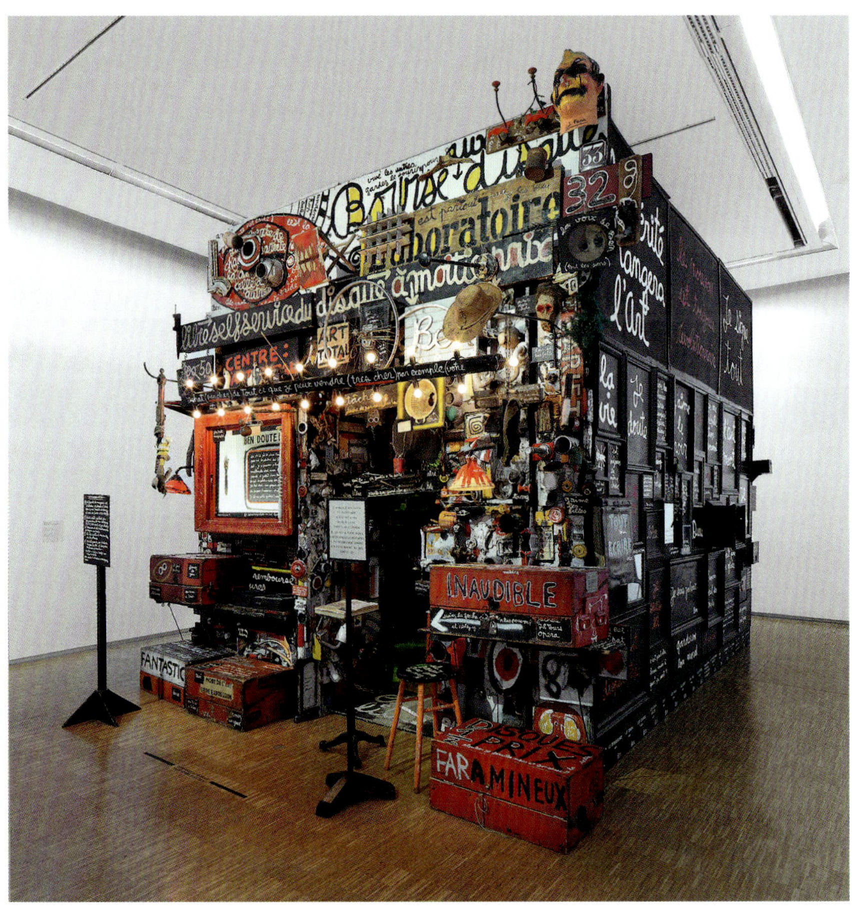

Figure 1 Ben (Ben Vautier) (born Naples, Italy, 1935; died Nice, France, 2024). *Le Magasin de Ben*, 1958–73. Mixed media; 402 × 446 × 596 cm (158¼ × 175⅝ × 234⅞ in.). Musée national d'art moderne, Centre Georges Pompidou, purchase, 1975, AM 1975-185.

There is nevertheless a key usefulness in bringing Ben Vautier and Jesse Howard together here, and that is their shared commitment to radical forthrightness. That commitment led both makers to prize a level, egalitarian address and to emphasize the value of speaking one's mind. Their streams of declarations and pronouncements each run clear because their beliefs, no matter the internal inconsistencies, were held transparently and bear the merit of an evident tenacity. Simplicity and sincerity characterize the selves that they made, for all the world to read and to see.

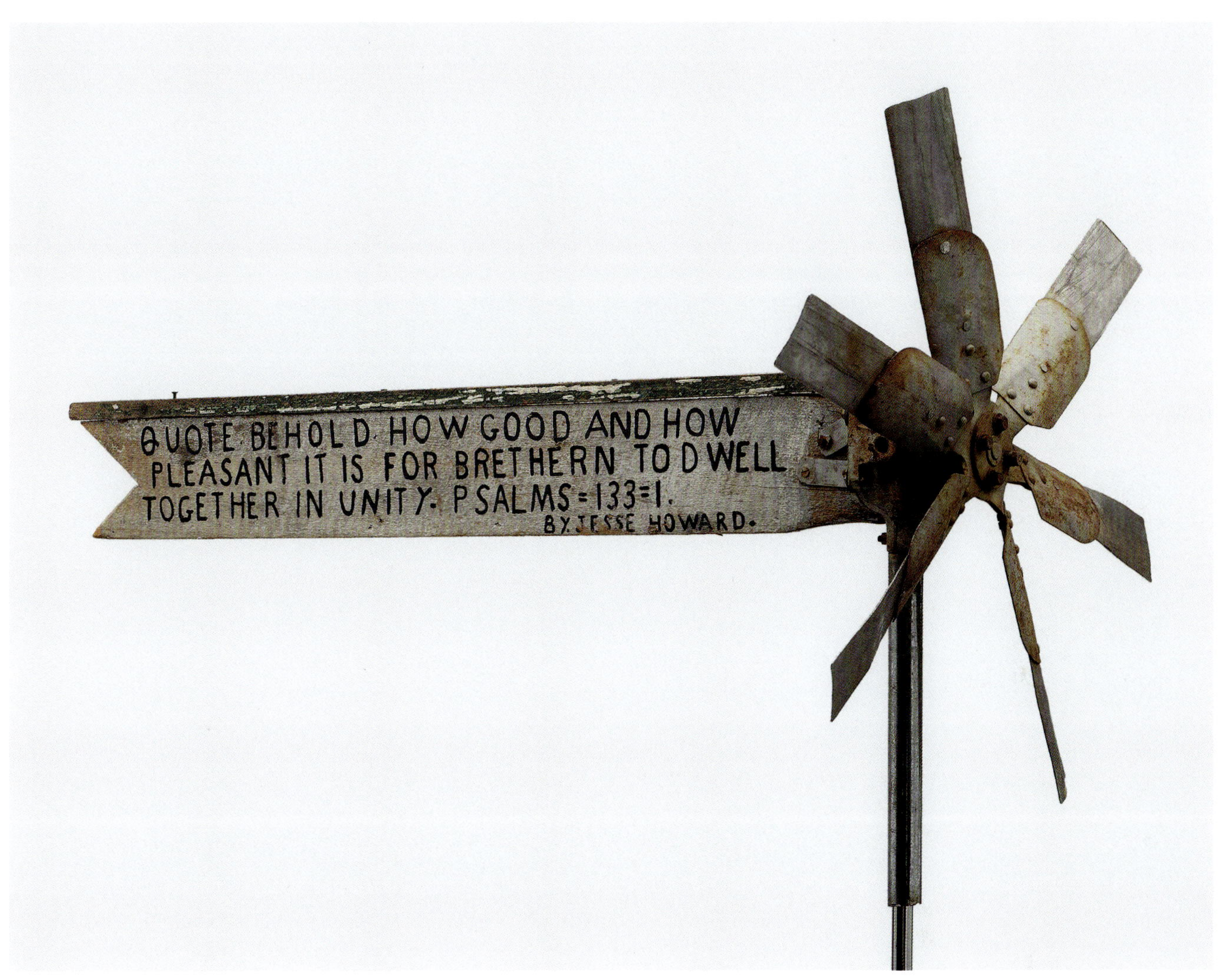

12
Untitled (Quote Behold How Good . . .)
1953–71
Paint on wood with found windmill wheel assembly and pipe
73.7 × 68.6 × 114.3 cm (29 × 27 × 45 in.)
The Art Institute of Chicago, gift of Richard and Ellen Sandor, 2025.617

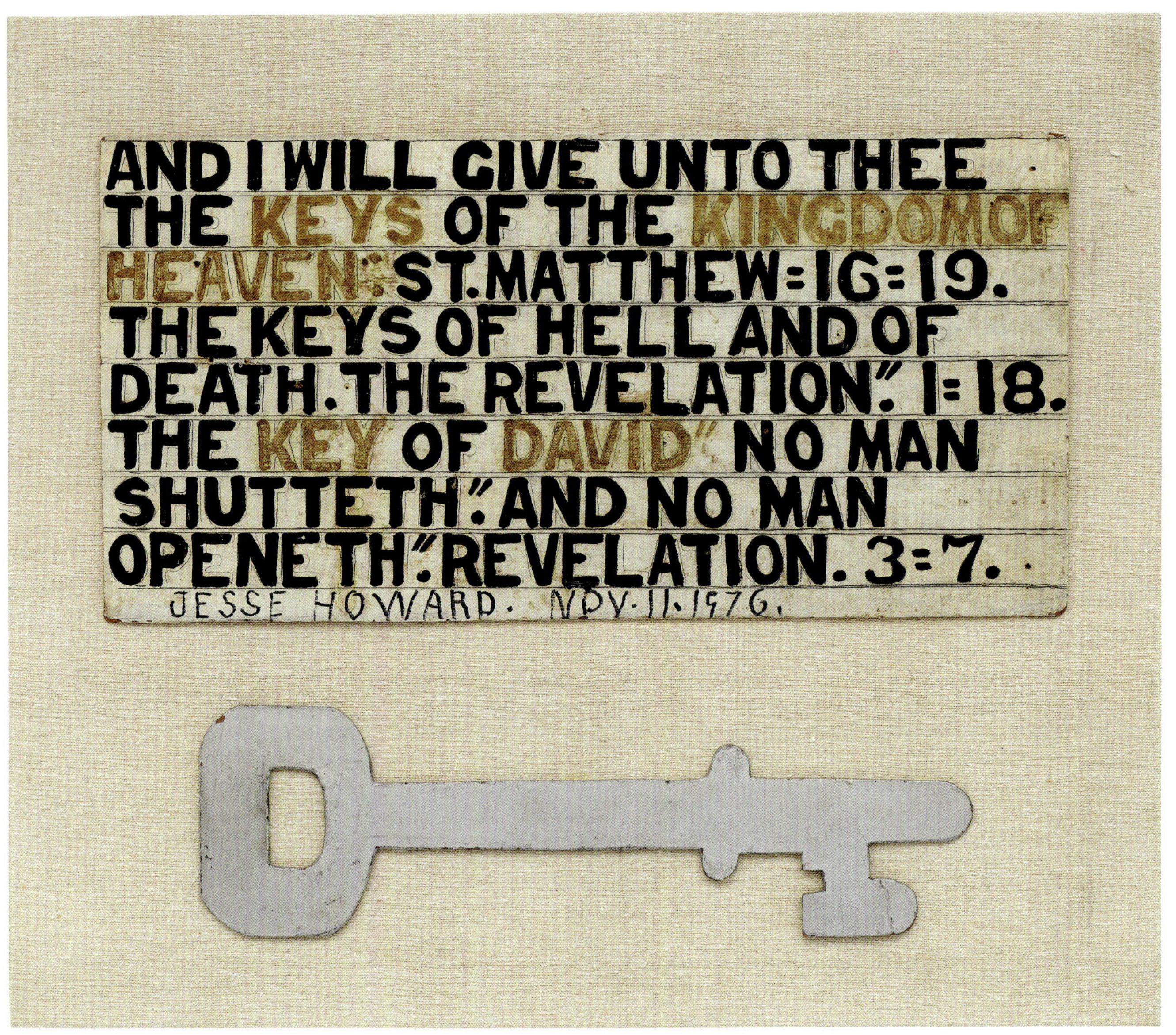

13
Untitled (And I Will Give Unto Thee . . .)
Nov. 11, 1976
Sign: paint and graphite on hardboard; key: paint on hardboard
Overall: 53.4 × 61 × 2.6 cm (21 × 24 × 1 in.); sign: 25.4 × 50.8 × 0.4 cm (10 × 20 × ⅛ in.); key: 10.7 × 40.7 × 0.4 cm (4 3⁄16 × 16 × ⅛ in.)
The Art Institute of Chicago, gift of Richard and Ellen Sandor, 2025.612

14
Untitled (St. Louis Globe. Fri. Dec. 30. 1960)
Jan. 30, 1962
Paint and graphite on metal
50.8 × 65.1 × 0.4 cm (20 × 25 ⅝ × ⅛ in.)
The Art Institute of Chicago, gift of Richard and Ellen Sandor, 2025.616

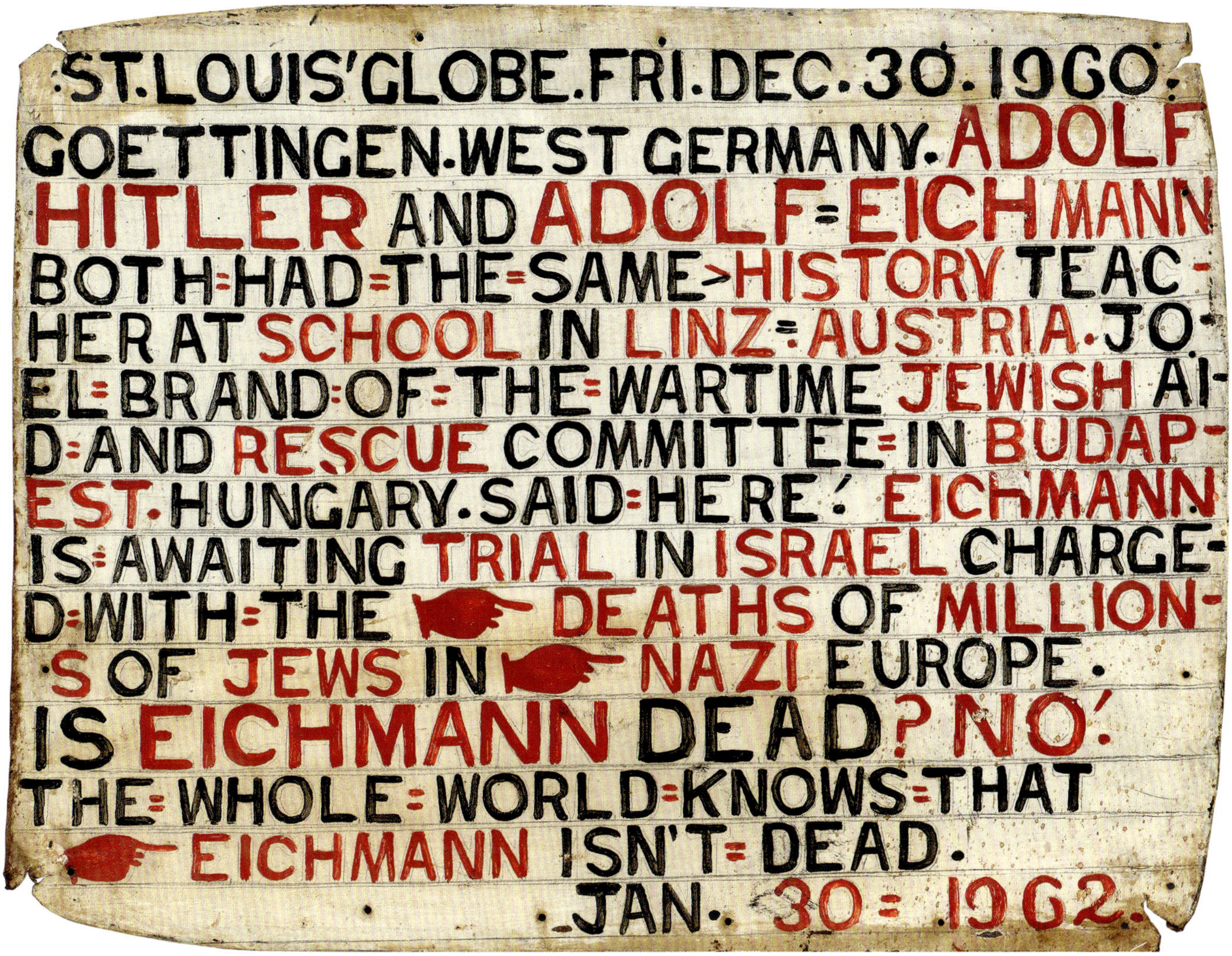

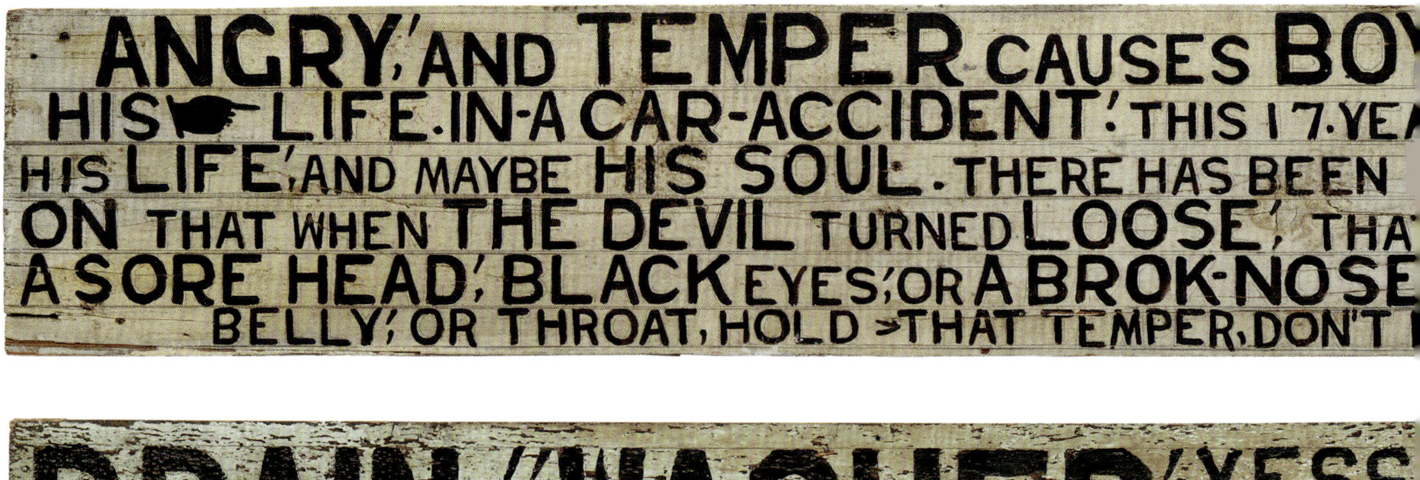

ANGRY; AND TEMPER CAUSES BOY
HIS LIFE. IN-A CAR-ACCIDENT! THIS 17. YEA
HIS LIFE; AND MAYBE HIS SOUL. THERE HAS BEEN
ON THAT WHEN THE DEVIL TURNED LOOSE; THA
A SORE HEAD; BLACK EYES; OR A BROK-NOSE
BELLY; OR THROAT, HOLD → THAT TEMPER, DON'T

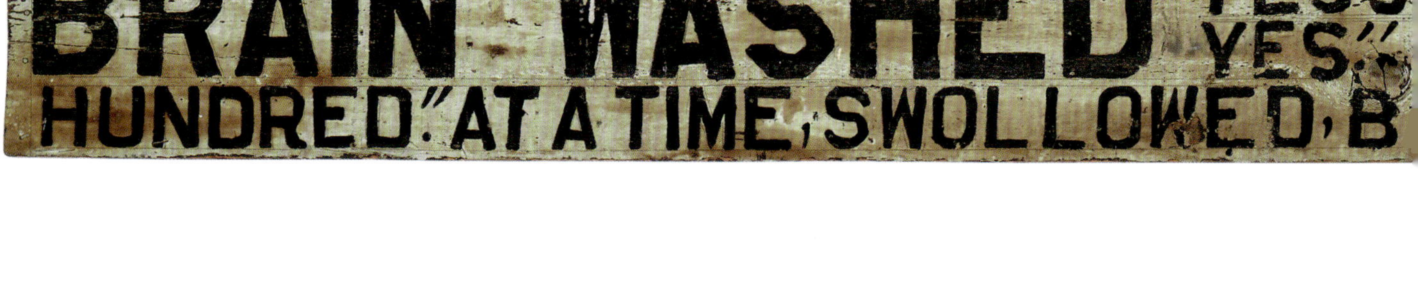

BRAIN "WASHED" YESS
YES."
HUNDRED." AT A TIME, SWOLLOWED, B

Top to bottom:

15
Untitled (Angry, And Temper Causes Boy To Loose His Life . . .)
1953–83
Paint and graphite on wood
25.1 × 134 × 2.1 cm (9 7⁄8 × 52 3⁄4 × 13⁄16 in.)
The Art Institute of Chicago, gift of Richard and Ellen Sandor, 2025.613

16
Untitled (Brain Washed Yesser . . .)
1953–71
Paint on wood
28.3 × 342.9 × 3.9 cm (11 1⁄8 × 135 × 1 1⁄2 in.)
The Art Institute of Chicago, gift of Richard and Ellen Sandor, 2025.614

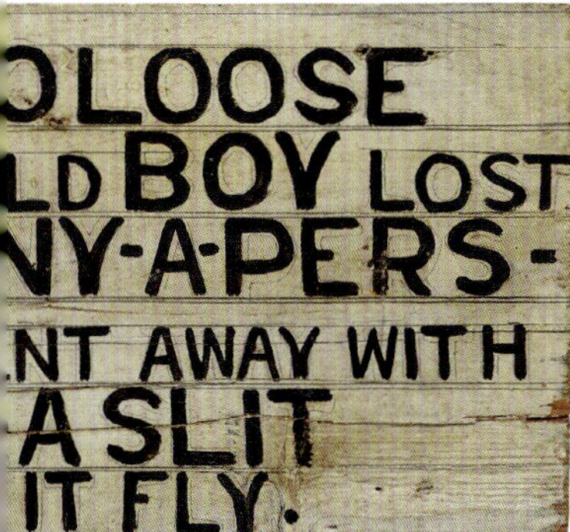

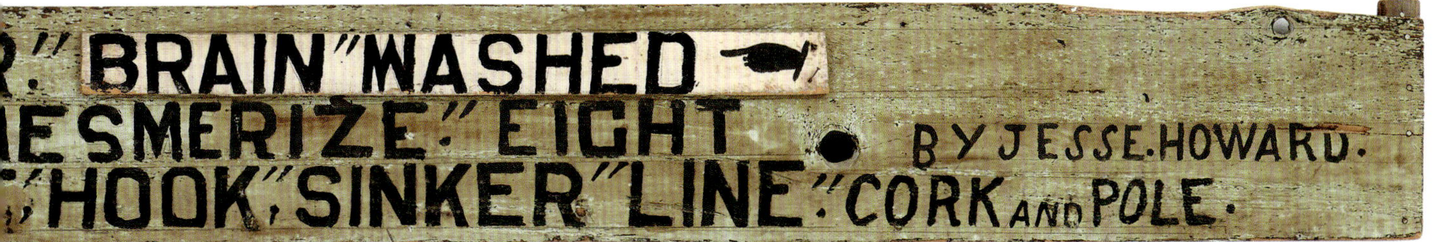

17
The Thorn Tree
1968
Paint and graphite on canvas with wood dowel
91.5 × 113.1 × 2 cm (36 × 44 ½ × ¾ in.)
The Art Institute of Chicago, gift of Richard and Ellen Sandor, 2025.618

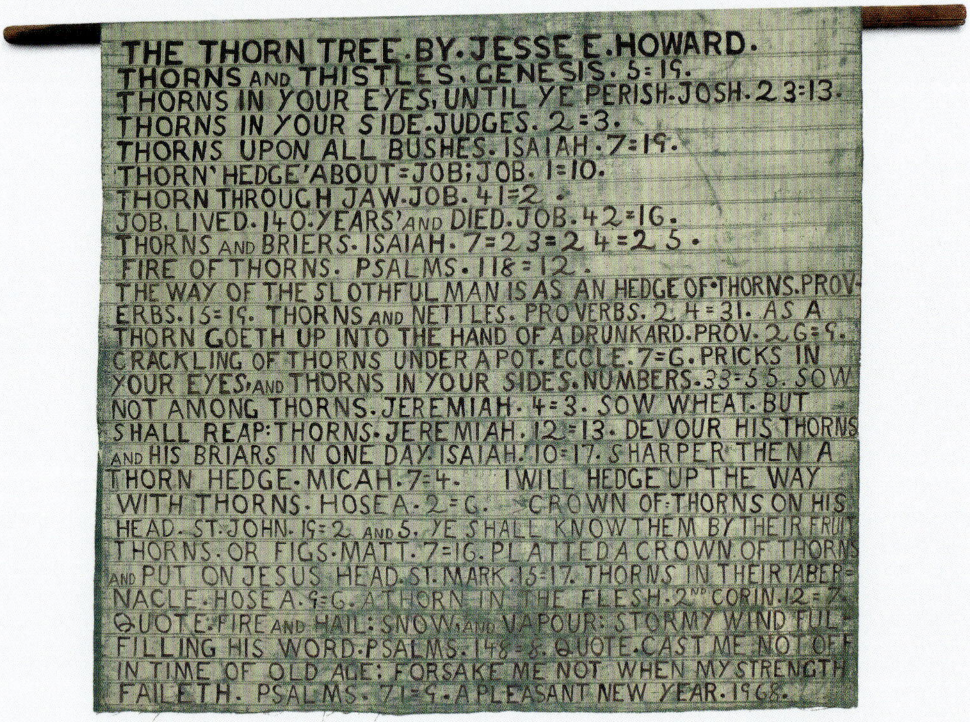

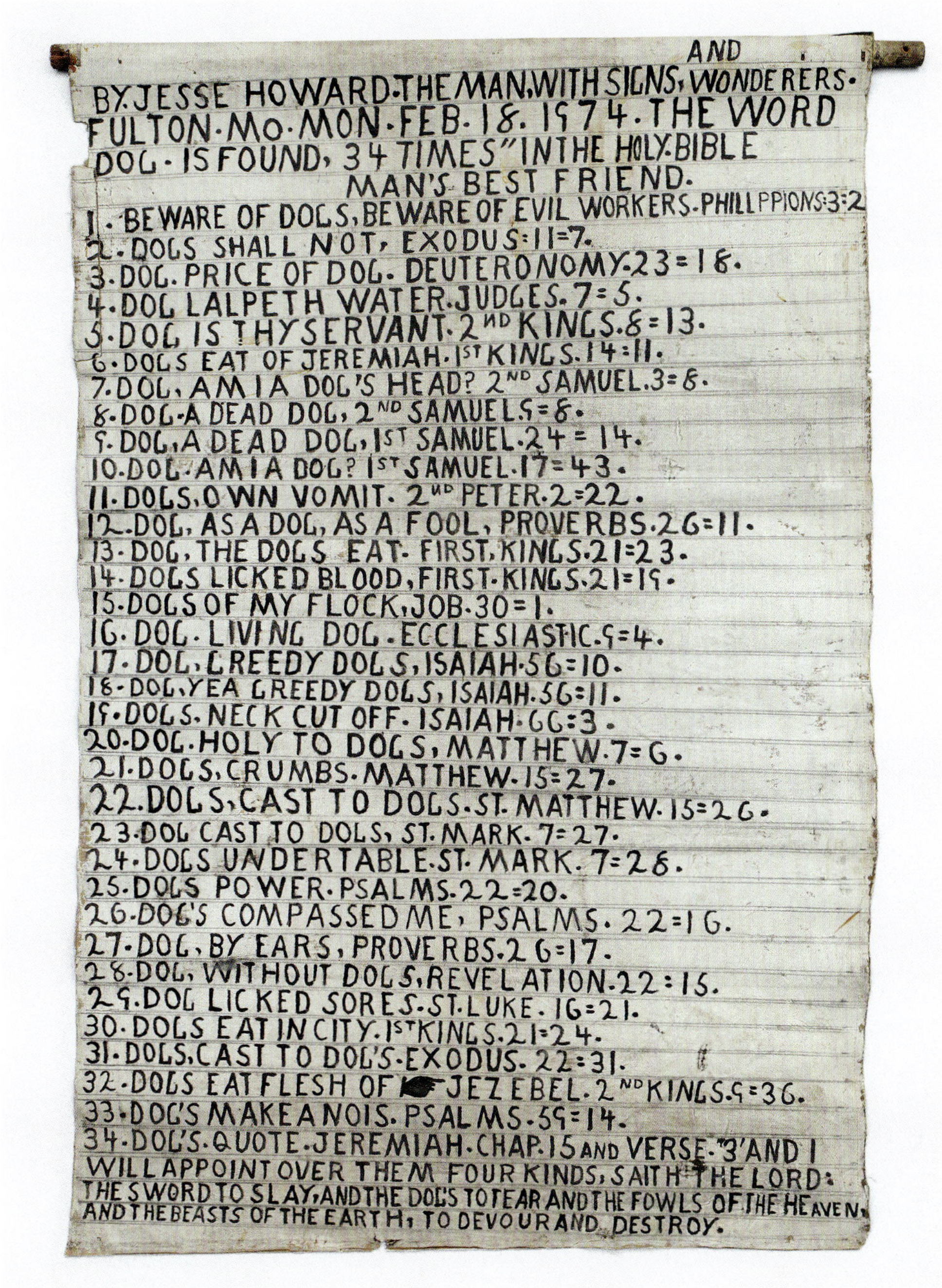

AND
BY JESSE HOWARD-THE MAN, WITH SIGNS, WONDERERS.
FULTON-Mo-MON-FEB-18. 1974. THE WORD
DOG-IS FOUND, 34 TIMES" IN THE HOLY BIBLE
MAN'S BEST FRIEND.
1. BEWARE OF DOGS, BEWARE OF EVIL WORKERS-PHILLPPIONS 3:2
2. DOGS SHALL NOT, EXODUS:11=7.
3. DOG. PRICE OF DOG. DEUTERONOMY.23=18.
4. DOG LALPETH WATER. JUDGES. 7=5.
5. DOG IS THY SERVANT. 2ND KINGS. 8=13.
6. DOGS EAT OF JEREMIAH. 1ST KINGS. 14=11.
7. DOG, AM I A DOG'S HEAD? 2ND SAMUEL. 3=8.
8. DOG-A DEAD DOG, 2ND SAMUEL 9=8.
9. DOG, A DEAD DOG, 1ST SAMUEL. 24=14.
10. DOG-AM I A DOG? 1ST SAMUEL. 17=43.
11. DOGS, OWN VOMIT. 2ND PETER. 2=22.
12. DOG, AS A DOG, AS A FOOL, PROVERBS. 26=11.
13. DOG, THE DOGS EAT. FIRST, KINGS. 21=23.
14. DOGS LICKED BLOOD, FIRST. KINGS. 21=19.
15. DOGS OF MY FLOCK, JOB. 30=1.
16. DOG. LIVING DOG. ECCLESIASTIC. 9=4.
17. DOG, GREEDY DOGS, ISAIAH. 56=10.
18. DOG, YEA GREEDY DOGS, ISAIAH. 56=11.
19. DOGS. NECK CUT OFF. ISAIAH. 66=3.
20. DOG. HOLY TO DOGS, MATTHEW. 7=6.
21. DOGS, CRUMBS. MATTHEW. 15=27.
22. DOGS, CAST TO DOGS. ST. MATTHEW. 15=26.
23. DOG CAST TO DOGS, ST. MARK. 7=27.
24. DOGS UNDER TABLE. ST. MARK. 7=28.
25. DOGS POWER. PSALMS. 22=20.
26. DOG'S COMPASSED ME, PSALMS. 22=16.
27. DOG, BY EARS, PROVERBS. 26=17.
28. DOG, WITHOUT DOGS, REVELATION. 22=15.
29. DOG LICKED SORES. ST. LUKE. 16=21.
30. DOGS EAT IN CITY. 1ST KINGS. 21=24.
31. DOGS, CAST TO DOG'S. EXODUS. 22=31.
32. DOGS EAT FLESH OF ☛ JEZEBEL. 2ND KINGS. 9=36.
33. DOG'S MAKE A NOIS. PSALMS. 59=14.
34. DOG'S. QUOTE. JEREMIAH. CHAP. 15 AND VERSE. "3" AND I
WILL APPOINT OVER THEM FOUR KINDS, SAITH THE LORD:
THE SWORD TO SLAY, AND THE DOG'S TO TEAR AND THE FOWLS OF THE HEAVEN,
AND THE BEASTS OF THE EARTH, TO DEVOUR AND DESTROY.

18
Man's Best Friend
Feb. 18, 1974
Paint and graphite on canvas with wood dowel
122 × 88.6 × 2.6 cm (48 × 34 ⅞ × 1 in.)
The Art Institute of Chicago, gift of Richard and Ellen Sandor, 2025.619

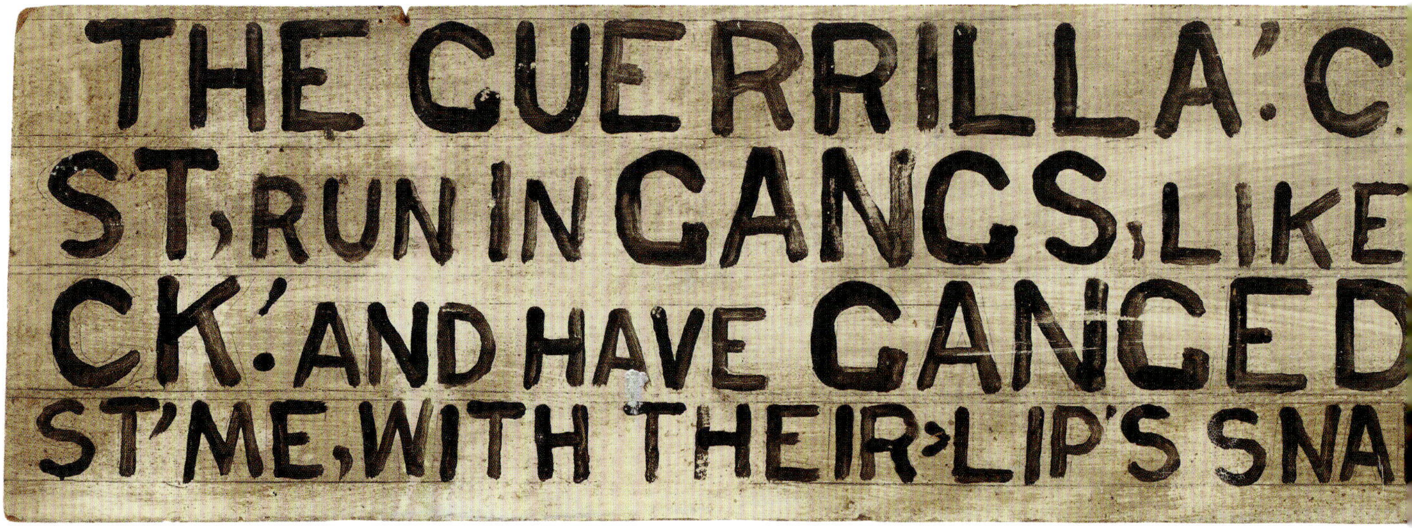

THE GUERRILLA'C
ST, RUN IN GANGS, LIKE
CK' AND HAVE GANGED
ST'ME, WITH THEIR·LIP'S SNA

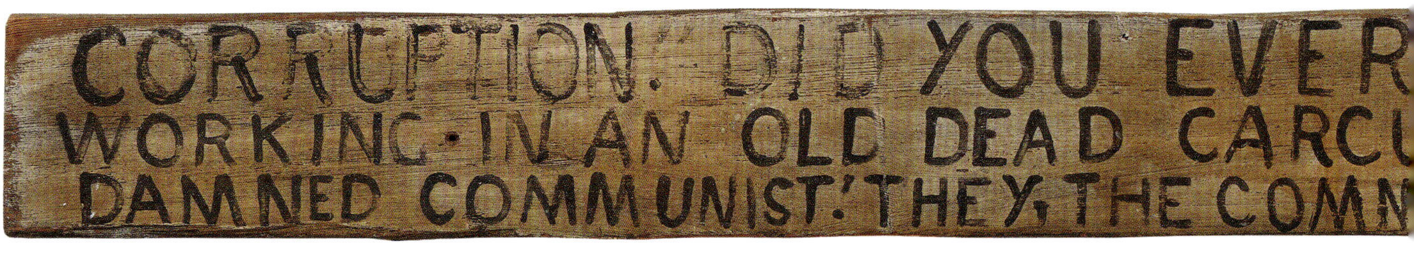

CORRUPTION: DID YOU EVER
WORKING·IN AN OLD DEAD CARCU
DAMNED COMMUNIST' THEY, THE COMMN

Top to bottom:

19
Untitled (The Guerilla. Communist …)
n.d.
Paint and graphite on hardboard
19.4 × 75 cm (7⅝ × 29½ in.)
Collection of Richard and Ellen Sandor

20
Untitled (Corruption. Did You Ever See A Ball Of Maggots …)
1953–83
Paint on wood
11.5 × 149.9 cm (4½ × 59 in.)
The Art Institute of Chicago, gift of Richard and Ellen Sandor, 2025.615

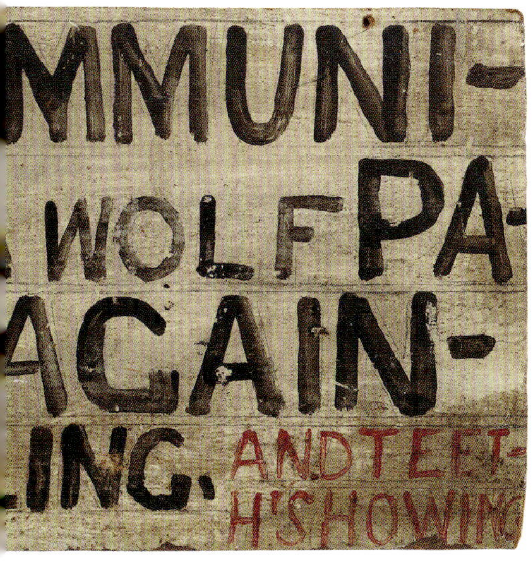

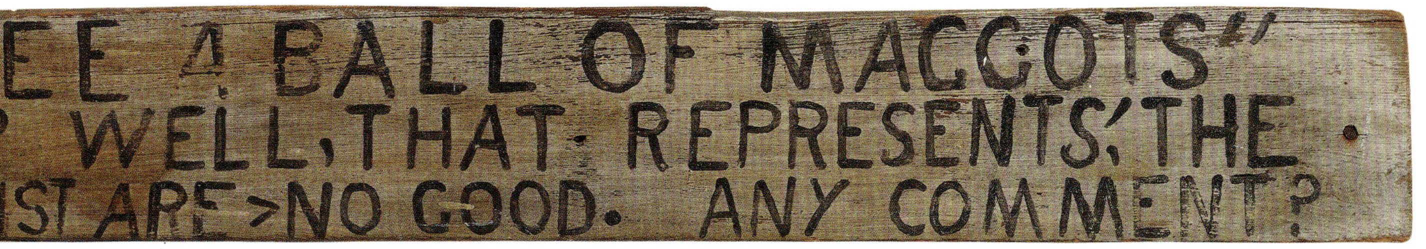

Annette Messager

Born Berck, France, 1943; active Paris

French sculptor and textile artist Annette Messager, who worked frequently with photographs in the 1970s and 1980s, located an edition of her early work Les Tortures Volontaires, *or* Voluntary Tortures, *while reorganizing her inventory in 2012. She published the work in a dedicated volume the following year, placing each of the images on a separate page. Messager wrote a preface to the book, reprinted here with minor edits for clarity.*

The text conveys Messager's intertwined aesthetic commitments to feminism and popular image production. She instantiates those twin commitments in part through the construction of multiple authorial identities—discrediting any notion of a female "essence" by making herself into many.[1] —MW

Les Tortures Volontaires (*Voluntary Tortures*) is part of a series of works from the early nineteen-seventies when I called myself Annette Messager, collector.

I was interested in the worthless arts. As a female artist at that time I was a worthless artist, a minority artist.

I was intent on highlighting this fact in my work. So, I sought out worthless domains and worked to draw attention to them, particularly women's territory, which was thought of as obscure and repressed.

Hence my predilection for popular art, proverbs, photography, fairy tales, embroidery, and Art Brut.

This attitude ran counter to the art of the nineteen-seventies, which was dominated by Minimalist and Conceptual Art.

I had no title, so I invented one for myself. That way, I became someone important, someone with a defined character. I found an identity through all those different personalities: Annette Messager, collector; Annette Messager, artist; Annette Messager, practical woman; Annette Messager, trickster; Annette Messager, peddler.

In her bedroom, Annette Messager collects, studies, and clips things out of books, newspapers, and magazines. She reassembles them in *Album-Collections*.

Les Tortures Volontaires consists of a wall installation of photos from the press and *Album-Collection No. 18*.[2]

Photographs of faces covered by masks and creams; bodies and thighs enclosed in awe-inspiring, infernal contraptions.

Electrostimulation, vibrating platforms, massage apparatuses, and a thousand other tortures worthy of Dante's *Inferno*.

At the same time, I was very interested visually by this material—the colors and *craquelures* of the various creams on the bodies—all these devices that are reminiscent of certain techniques that the body-art artists used in the same period.

A few months ago I was putting some things away in a closet that I rarely use—I hate it, because it's such a mess—and, quite by chance, I found eighty-one photographs that I had completely forgotten about, prints I had made in 1972. They were part of my piece *Les Tortures Volontaires*.

And that gave me the idea of suggesting it for this book with Hatje Cantz.

These days, people's bodies and faces are remodeled, regenerated, transformed, and fantasized—all in accordance with socially defined standards.

Unlike wines, which change over time and acquire their bouquet with age, we humans never stop struggling against the natural processes of time.

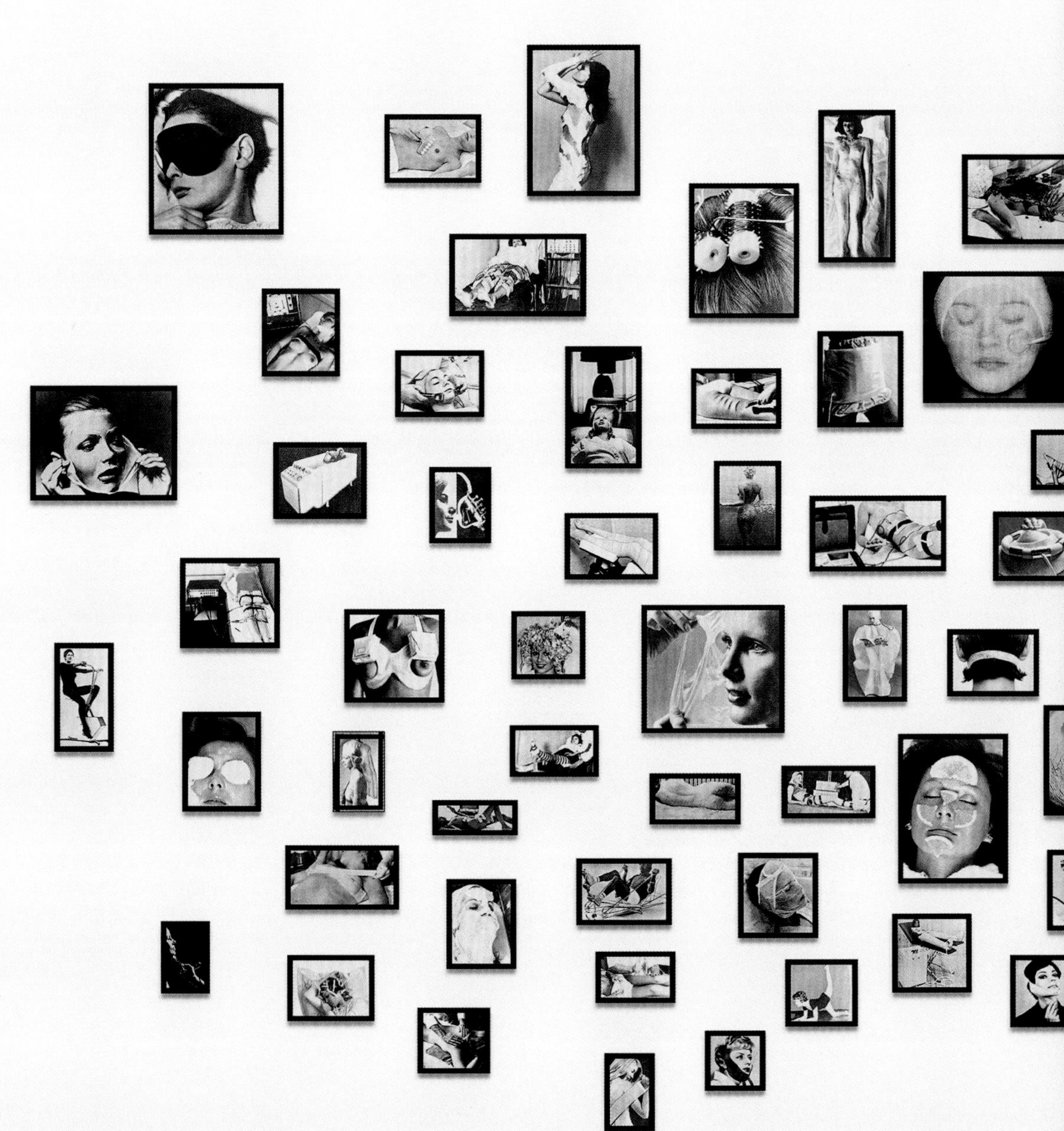

21
Les Tortures Volontaires (Voluntary Tortures): Album-Collection No. 18
1972
83 gelatin silver prints
Installation dimensions variable
The Art Institute of Chicago, gift of Richard and Ellen Sandor, 2025.876.1–83

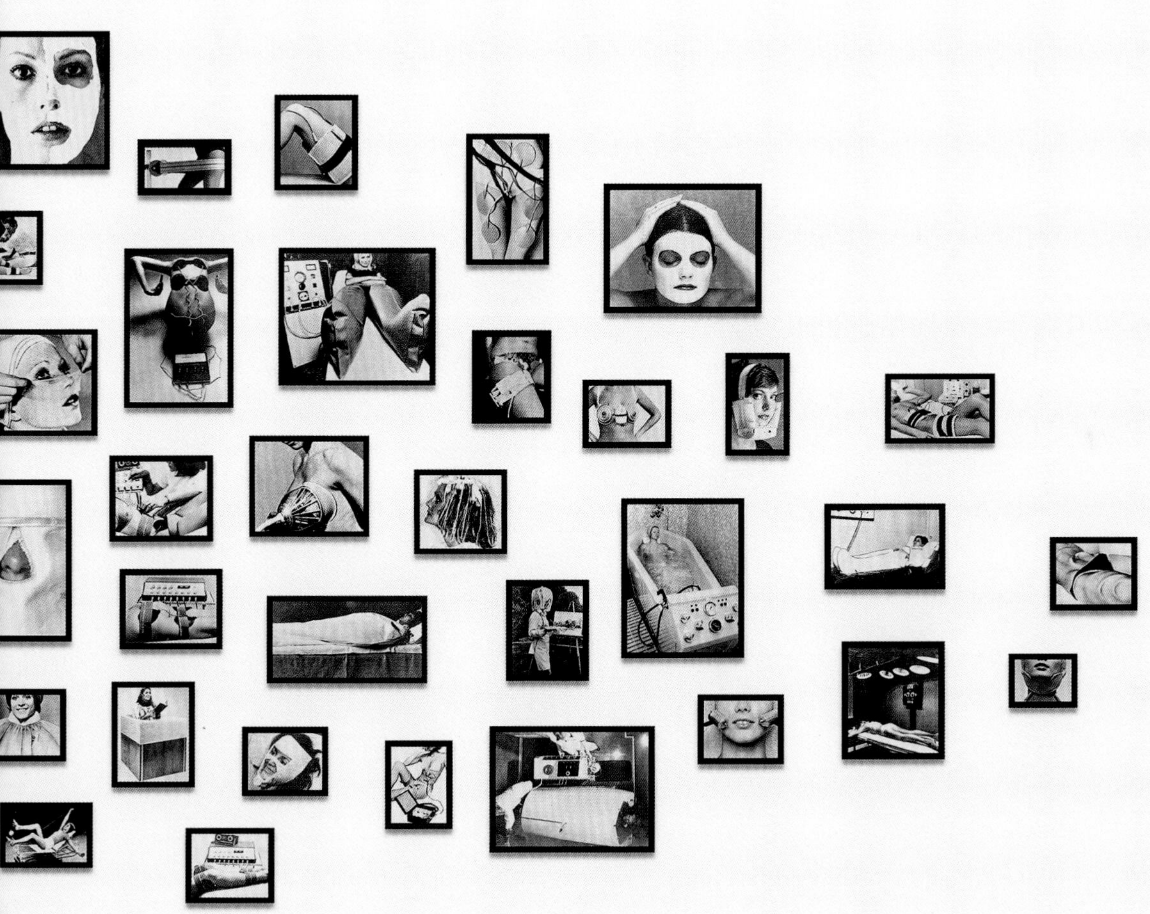

Mr. Imagination

Born Chicago, 1948; died Atlanta, 2012

As with several artists in this book, Mr. Imagination did not make so much as remake his identity. Born Gregory Warmack, he changed his name at the age of thirty after suffering a nearly fatal gunshot to his stomach. With this rebirth came a deepening of spiritual investment and a broadening of impulses he had had as a child toward visual play and creativity: "The assault left him hospitalized and comatose for six weeks. During that interval, he had what he described as an out-of-body experience in which he saw visions of ancient cultures. It took him a year to recover from his injuries."[1] Mr. Imagination henceforth undertook to transform castoff, common materials into transcendent objects invested with ritual meaning.[2]

Mr. I, as he wanted to be called, took up carving in molded sandstone, a byproduct of glass and other industrial casting that could be readily salvaged in the Chicago area, where he lived for much of his life. These works often evoked Indigenous tribal masks and Biblical or royal figures, as for example in a collaboration with Ellen Sandor (fig. 1). The Sandors came to his work through Chicago dealer Carl Hammer, who represented a number of the artists discussed in this volume.

Warmack began using bottle caps in about 1990 and soon made them into a signature material. In his work *Bottlecap Fish* (pl. 22), which appeared in his final show with the Hammer Gallery in 2002, tops from bottles of Smirnoff vodka fashion the body of a flying fish and also elevate the base on which it rests. Spirituality does not equate to piety—the fish smiles as it soars, drunk on cheap liquor. But there is a regal or otherworldly aspiration in even the humblest of Warmack's creations, and in his self-conception, as an obituary writer makes clear: "In one memorable photo, he wears a

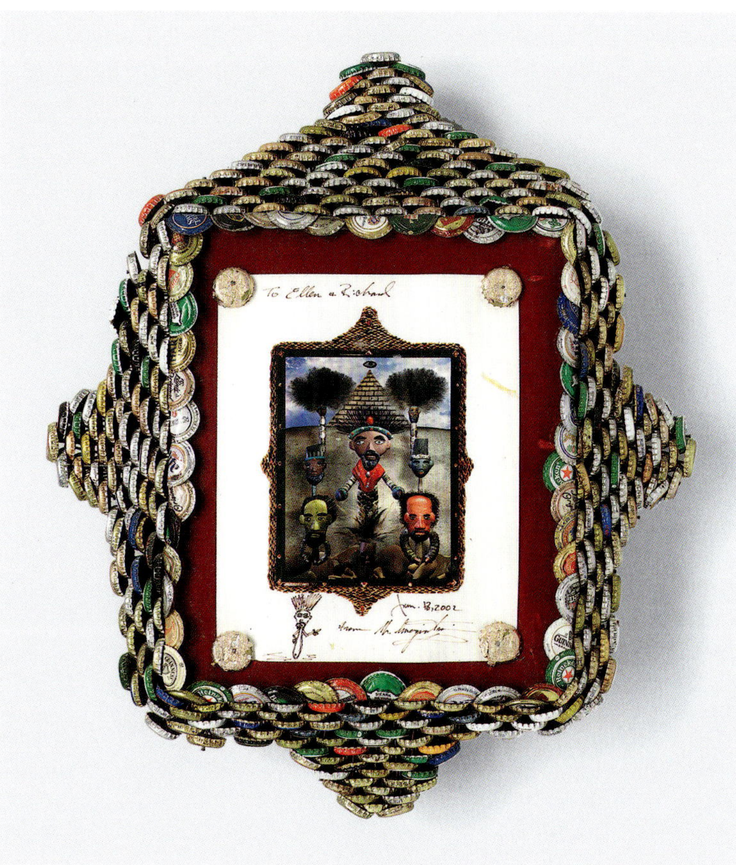

Figure 1 (art)^n (founded Chicago, 1983), Ellen Sandor (born Brooklyn, 1942; active Chicago), and Mr. Imagination. *The Third Eye of Mr. I*, 2002. Inkjet print, in artist's wood frame with bottle caps; 25.4 × 20.4 cm (10 × 8 in.). Collection of Richard and Ellen Sandor.

bottle-cap suit and hat, while sitting on a throne festooned with bottle caps and holding a staff decorated with the caps."[3]

Hammer recalled the essential element of Warmack's conception of art to be "his belief in the spiritual energies possessed by his pieces, which were infused both in the creation process and by the collaborative contributions of the spirit of people both living and dead."[4] With this characterization in mind, the diminutive flying fish sculpture calls to mind Ga fantasy coffins from southern Ghana, made from about the 1950s through the present day by sculptors such as Joseph Tetteh-Ashong, known as Paa Joe (see fig. 2). Such sculptures, commissioned in recent decades by affluent Ghanaian Christians as well as for the international art market, merge symbols of a profession, such as fishmonger, with markers of social position and familial identity for the deceased.[5] The coffins—which in many cases are requested to symbolize entombment rather than serve it in a practical sense—join professional, personal, and spiritual dimensions

Figure 2 Workshop of Paa Joe (Joseph Tetteh-Ashong) (born Akwapim, Ghana, 1947; active Pobiman, near Accra). *Fish Coffin*, c. 1970s–80s. Wood and enamel; 135 × 270 × 70 cm (53⅛ × 105 5/16 × 27 9/16 in.). Museum für Sepulkralkultur, Kassel, Sammlung Hermann Krause, gift of Antje Hegge, Cologne, M 2018/13.18.

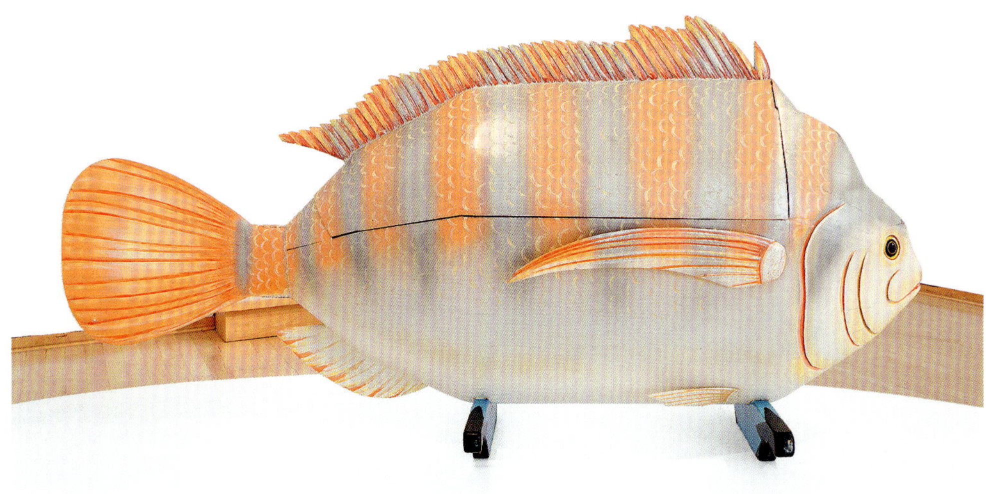

into a holistic commemorative container that suggests freedom of movement and of mind. This seems precisely the aim of *Bottlecap Fish* by Mr. Imagination. Stepping back from a comparison of individual works, one can say that Mr. Imagination's insistence on repurposing castoff materials and his drive to educate and connect through art made circulation and recycling into eminently creative lines of movement.

22
Bottlecap Fish
2002
Found aluminum bottle caps and acrylic on plaster, wood, and tin
21.6 × 29.3 × 10.8 cm (8½ × 11½ × 4¼ in.)
The Art Institute of Chicago, gift of Richard and Ellen Sandor, 2025.620

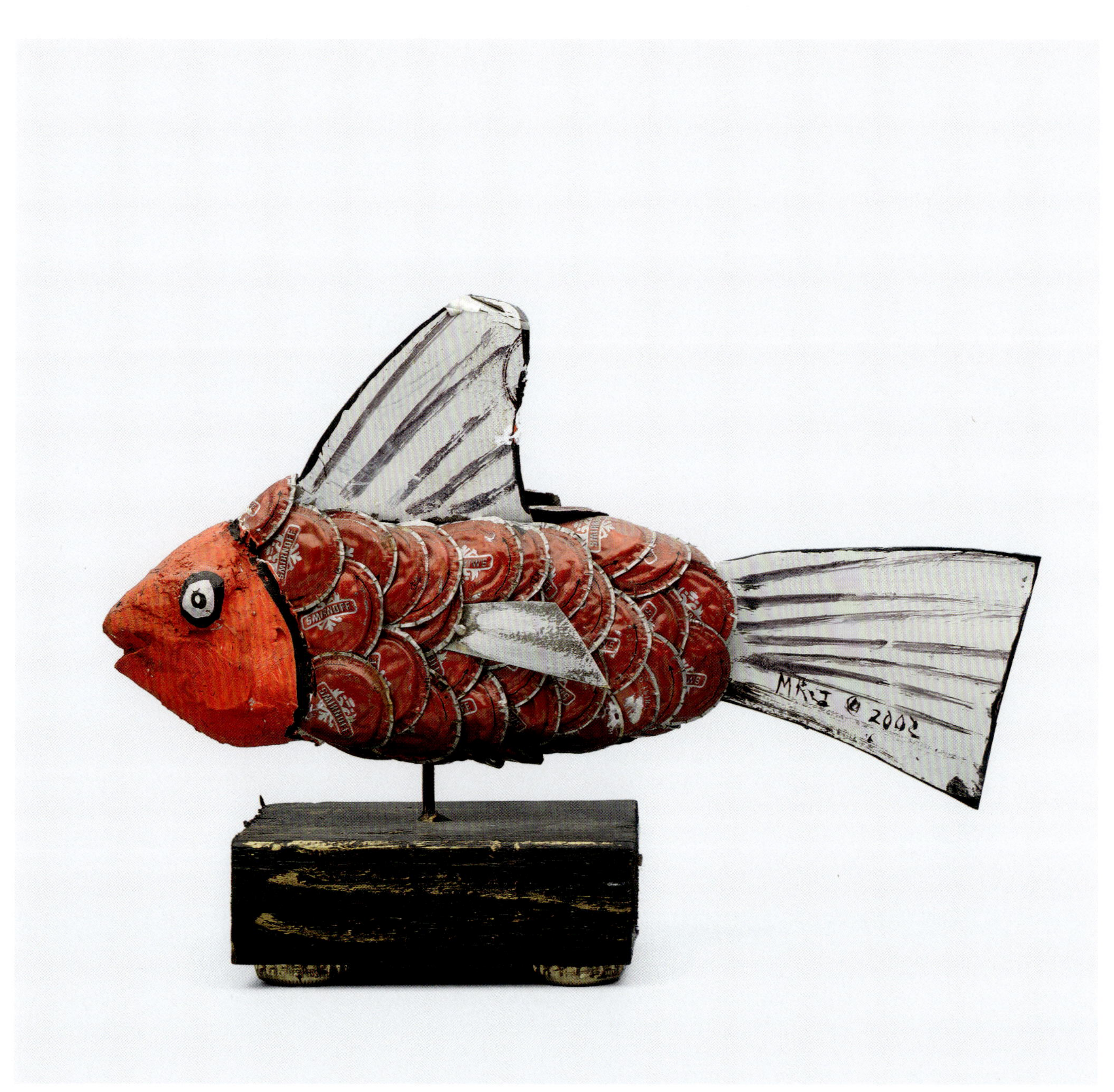

Martín Ramírez

Born Jalisco, Mexico, 1895; died Auburn, CA, 1963

Rather than a "self, made," it might be better to describe the art of transnational migrant worker Martín Ramírez as the result of a personhood unmade through involuntary institutionalization. Arrested and hospitalized in California through coercive measures at the age of thirty-six, and imprisoned in seclusion in that state until his death, Ramírez turned to art after repeated attempts to escape. His production of drawings, using a material inventiveness that seems propelled by ambition and desperation in equal measure, was actively fostered by personnel at DeWitt State Hospital, his second place of internment (1948–63). Works by Ramírez began to be exhibited in those years as well, although Ramírez himself was not named nor invited to see the exhibitions, let alone participate in their organization. His art gained major recognition ten years after his death, in part thanks to the efforts of art dealer Phyllis Kind, then based in Chicago, and artist Jim Nutt, who had trained at the School of the Art Institute of Chicago. Nutt and his partner, artist Gladys Nilsson, once owned the drawing reproduced here.

The details of Ramírez's history and the sources of his imagery in the Jalisco highlands, where he was born and started adulthood as an impoverished rancher with a wife and four children, were brought to light by Víctor M. Espinosa in an assiduously researched monograph, Martín Ramírez: Framing His Life and Art.[1] *Espinosa argues that Ramírez's art "is not a passive manifestation of mental illness but an example of resistance, survival, and artistic agency from the perspective of a subaltern subjectivity." The author has generously permitted publication of an excerpt from the introduction to his book.* — MW

In 1925, like thousands of Mexicans, Ramírez went to look for work in the United States, leaving his family at home in a small rural community in Mexico. In January 1931, at the age of thirty-six, he was detained by police in Stockton, California, emotionally upset and in very bad physical condition. After a medical evaluation, he was diagnosed with chronic depression and interned in a crowded psychiatric hospital. After spending several months under observation and unaided by an interpreter, he was diagnosed with catatonic schizophrenia. During the clinical evaluation, he limited himself to simply repeating that he did not speak English and that he was not "mad." In those years, for somebody in his situation, his diagnosis meant a life sentence. He was never released. After thirty-two years of seclusion, he died in 1963 at the age of sixty-eight.

Ramírez was saved from anonymity because after several attempts to escape from the psychiatric hospital, he began to draw obsessively. He worked every day, crouched on the floor over enormous sheets of paper he constructed out of scraps. He patiently glued together the paper he received from the hospital, along with any he found in the garbage cans, using glue he made by mixing saliva with potato. His art materials consisted only of pencils, crayons, shoe polish, red juice extracted from fruits, the charcoal from used matchsticks, and a paste he made by mixing some of the raw materials with oatmeal, his own saliva, and even his own sputum.... Ramírez demonstrated no other interests and did not participate in ward activities; and perhaps because he was able to speak only very little English, he seemed uninterested in talking to other patients. The exact number of drawings that Ramírez completed during his life is unknown: Many were destroyed by the personnel of the two hospitals where he was confined. The 450 or so drawings known to exist today were collected and preserved by two men: a Sacramento painter and professor of art and psychology who sporadically provided him with paper, pencils, and crayons, and the physician in charge of the ward where Ramírez was secluded during the last years of his life.

The content of Ramírez's drawings shows that he was driven by a strong need for expression, communication, and recognition. His work is filled with nostalgic scenes of his life in Mexico, including recognizable churches of the towns where he lived, local religious icons, the rural landscape, laborers, common fauna of Mexico, his own domestic animals, people dancing, men making music with a violin and a *guitarrón*, scenes of bullfighting, and, especially, horsemen and horsewomen. The content of his work suggests that drawing became a prime means of preserving his identity, keeping his memory alive, and trying to give sense and order to an external and internal world in crisis. Ramírez's drawings are characterized by their monumental size, despite his chronic shortage of materials, and unusual, layered texture. But what has most attracted those who have been exposed to Ramírez's drawings since the 1950s is his ability to construct a very personal visual language through a balance between tradition and modernity, and through a successful integration of the figurative and the abstract.

The stigma of mental illness and Ramírez's lack of formal training have made it difficult to classify his work. His drawings were first exhibited anonymously in the 1950s and 1960s as examples of "psychotic art." Since his work entered the art market in 1973, his drawings have been shown in exhibitions of naive art, traditional and contemporary American folk art, *art brut*, outsider art, self-taught art, and vernacular art. Ramírez is a cross-border artist who produced all his work in a transnational third space, that is, far away from his homeland, completely marginalized from society in California, without being part of any immigrant or Latino artistic community. Only in recent years has Ramírez become a symbol of the Mexican immigrant experience and a source of inspiration for many Latinx artists and writers in the United States.

It was not until the last two decades of the twentieth century that the mainstream art world began taking serious interest in what is now popularly called "outsider" art. Today, this genre makes up a part of the contemporary fragmented and globalized art world. Certainly, Ramírez's life story is an inspiring example of perseverance, endurance, and powerful artistic production created under extreme and difficult conditions. The unlikely survival of his work, the myths about his life that were created and promoted by some art dealers, and the process through which his drawings have increased in both aesthetic and material value present a fascinating story. Yet the politics behind the process of Ramírez's artistic recognition and legitimization by mainstream institutions pose many questions regarding the commodification of works produced by marginalized creators and the reproduction of hierarchies in the contemporary art world. When, for whom, and under what conditions do objects produced by an outsider become art? How does an outsider become recognized as an artist? What does Ramírez's work lose in the process of decontextualization and recontextualization that is part of any mainstream assimilation?

23
Untitled (Jinete with Red Shirt No. 3)
1950–55
Graphite, tempera, and crayon on 2 sheets of cream wove paper, pieced
72.5 × 61 cm (28 9⁄16 × 24 1⁄16 in.)
The Art Institute of Chicago, gift of Richard and Ellen Sandor, 2025.1002

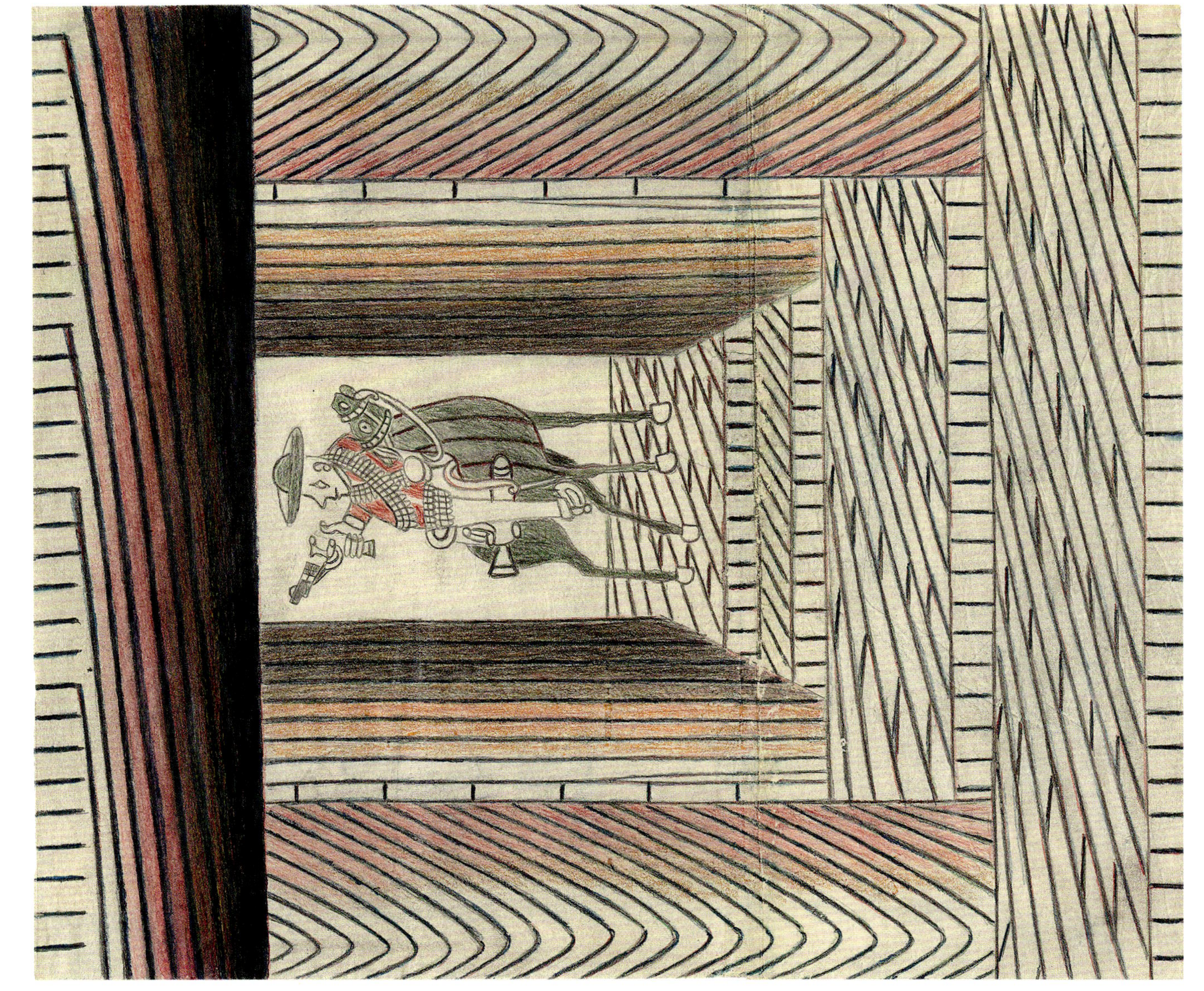

Cindy Sherman

Born Glen Ridge, NJ, 1954; active New York

Among the best-known artists of the last fifty years, Cindy Sherman has explored with great inventiveness the intersections of the specific and the generic that set the terms for selfhood in a media-saturated society. Working as cast, crew, and art director of her own productions, and appearing alone in her images, Sherman at once inhabits and offers for analysis various types or characters: film stars, centerfolds, clowns, hags, society ladies, and many others. Since the series *Untitled Film Stills* (1977–80), her works have been left without titles, the better to invite viewers to project their own investments onto personages who hold in tension the singular and the stereotypical.

Untitled (Lucy) (pl. 24) dates from before the breakthrough *Untitled Film Stills* and as such belongs to Sherman's formative beginnings as a college student in Buffalo, New York. A catalogue raisonné covering the approximately thirty-month period between 1975 and Sherman's move to New York in 1977 has yielded fifty-nine works, including this one, that demonstrate the artist's often labor-intensive commitment to performance and costuming. A 1976 theater-piece-cum-installation-work called—appropriately for this book—*A Play of Selves* epitomizes these explorations: A Broken Woman, as the portmanteau character, and multiple subsidiary allegorical figures interact across seventy scenes involving nearly 250 photographic cutouts, each clothed, staged, and photographed by Sherman with herself as the sole actor.[1]

Lucy was something other than a staging of self or a melodrama—it could be called a one-night stand. Gabriele Schor, author of the catalogue raisonné on Sherman's early works, quoted Sherman on her "occasional" practice of appearing publicly in costume: "Originally, I did it in Buffalo only a couple of times.... It was a spontaneous thing. Maybe I would be playing in my studio and there would be an opening in a couple of hours and I would just stay in character." Speaking specifically of her impromptu manifestation as Lucy, Sherman recalls: "One day I was playing around in my bedroom, which was my studio, and turned into Lucille Ball. I went out into our communal area where people were watching TV. Everyone was laughing and then somebody said, 'Oh, you should go document this. Go to the photo booth and take a picture.'"[2]

Everything about this image seems exceptional. It was not part of a series or installation but a one-off creation. Sherman did not aim for the generic or stereotypical but impersonated the most famous character of a celebrity actor, and eventually named that character in the title (which Sherman bestowed only in 2001, long after she had taken to calling all her works *Untitled*). That Sherman succeeded eerily well at the likeness is evidenced by her friends' reaction and further supported by commercial portraits of Ball in her heyday (see fig. 1); note that Sherman also owns work by Lee Godie, who was likewise inspired by past film and television stars (see fig. 2). Finally, Sherman did not make the photograph in her studio/bedroom, but in a photobooth, following a pastime that her Buffalo cohort regularly enjoyed as "a casual thing."[3] To keep to the language of cinema, we could say that *Untitled (Lucy)* is an "outtake" that shows the setting for Sherman's early work more than the work itself. And yet it has qualities that connect it to Sherman's greatest insights and her singular courage. Principally, these have to do with aging in the public eye, specifically as a woman.

The very first image reproduced in the catalogue raisonné, made by a preteen Sherman, already signals her attraction for old age. A family photograph, dated to about 1966, shows Sherman and a friend on the street as color-coordinated grannies, a character Sherman adopted for Halloween that year as well.[4] Children may often play at being their grandparents, but Sherman recalls that, as the youngest child and with two of her four siblings out of the house from around the time of her birth, she has readily identified with older people throughout her life. This identification was perhaps cemented through her childhood discovery of a trove of clothes worn by her grandmother in the 1920s.

To inhabit the past in one's youth is the stuff of playacting; the stakes change as one enters middle age. *Untitled #580* (pl. 25) belongs to a series of twenty photographs included in Sherman's first show of new work after she turned sixty, presented at her longtime gallery Metro Pictures in New York. The series centers grandly posed film divas: "a group of 1920s Hollywood actresses, toiling under the star system, who are [now] rather long in the tooth. Yet, they're posing as though they're still in their prime in front of hallucinatory, painterly sets teetering on the edge of unreality."[5]

Sherman made the series "after coming to terms with health issues and getting older," as she shared in an interview

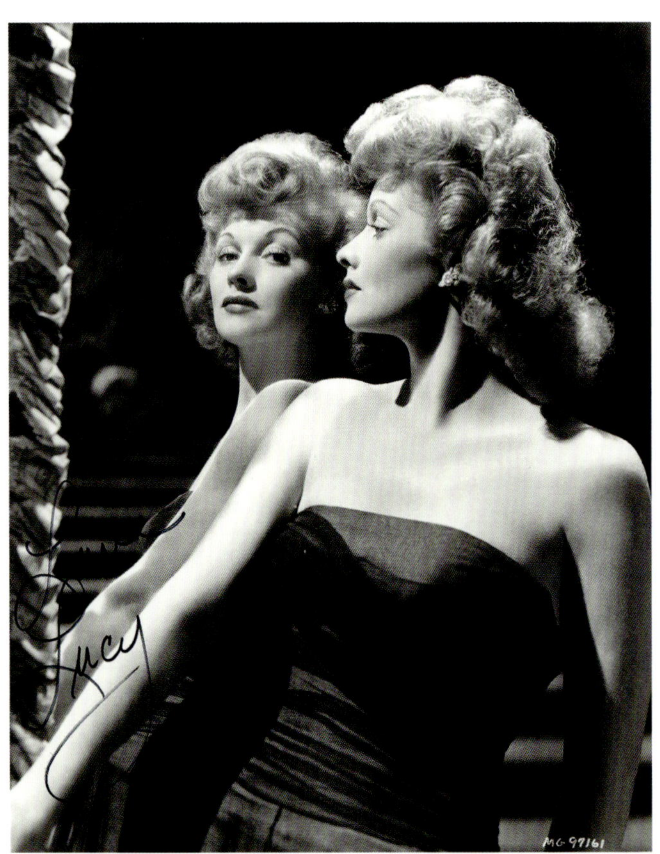

Figure 1 László Willinger (born Budapest, 1909; died Los Angeles, 1989). *Lucille Ball*, c. 1950. Gelatin silver print; 24.2 × 18.8 cm (9 9⁄16 × 7 3⁄8 in.). The Art Institute of Chicago, gift of Richard and Ellen Sandor, 2025.887.

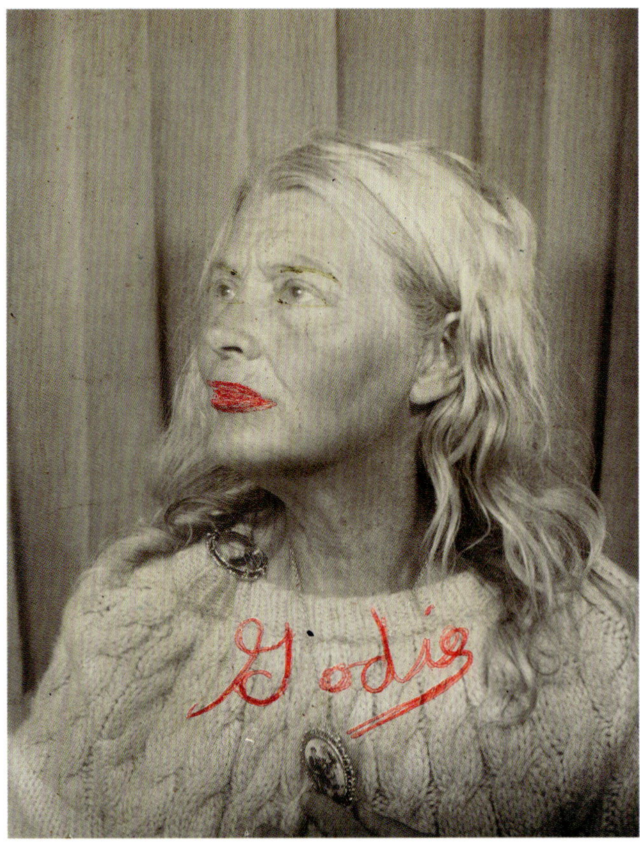

Figure 2 Lee Godie (born Chicago, 1908; died Plato Center, IL, 1994). *Lee and Cameo on a Chair Sincerily Lee Godie*, 1970s. Gelatin silver print with ink; 12.1 × 9.6 cm (4 3⁄4 × 3 3⁄4 in.). The Art Institute of Chicago, gift of Richard and Ellen Sandor, 2025.873.

24
Untitled (Lucy)
1975, printed 2001
Chromogenic print
25.4 × 20.4 cm (10 × 8 in.)
The Art Institute of Chicago, gift of Richard and Ellen Sandor, 2025.877

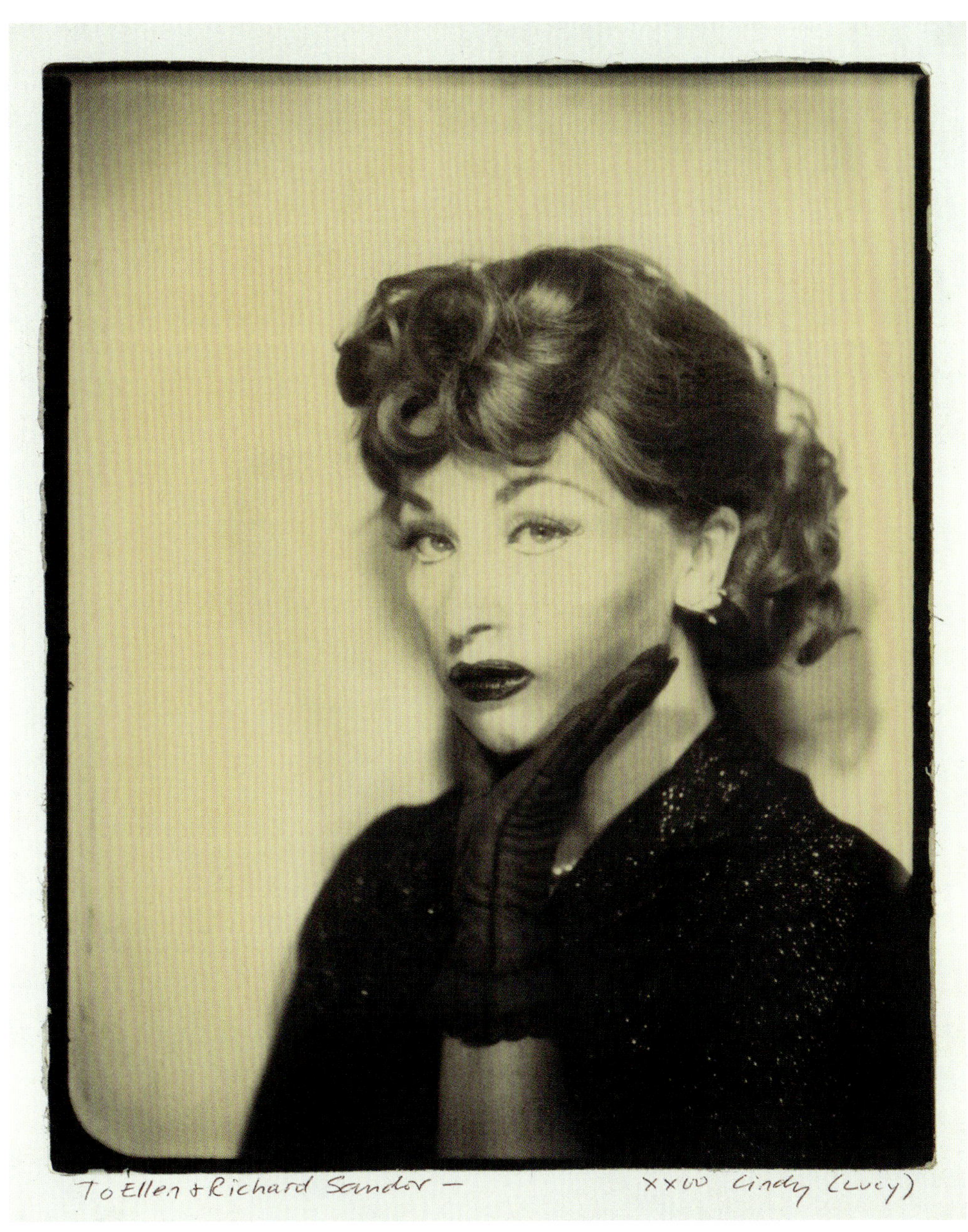

shortly before the show. "I relate so much to these women," Sherman continued: "They look like they've been through a lot, and they're survivors." Whereas in her younger days, Sherman avowed "trying to obliterate myself in the images," in the series from 2016—and in fact several others she has made over the past fifteen years—Sherman considers how "I, as an older woman, am struggling with the idea of being an older woman."[6]

All of which returns us to Sherman's brief turn as Lucille Ball one evening in 1975. Sherman evidently had foremost in mind Ball's character in *I Love Lucy*, the hit television show that ran from 1951 to 1957 and which Sherman—an obsessive TV-watching child—undoubtedly saw in daytime reruns that aired until 1967.[7] Ball, like Sherman, tested stereotypes and broke with them on-screen and off: in her on- and off-screen marriage to Cuban musician Desi Arnaz; in the show's throughline plot of a wife humorously yet persistently trying to escape the box of 1950s homemaker conformism; and by forming a production company with Arnaz that grew through *I Love Lucy* into a TV empire, and which she later ran on her own. (As head of Desilu Productions, Ball brought about *The Untouchables*, *Star Trek*, and *Mission: Impossible*, an impressive record of talent-spotting.)[8]

Sherman may not have known that Lucille Ball—actor, producer, and studio executive—worked as a "one-woman show" in an exact analogue to her own nascent practice. But she certainly reflected from early adulthood on the seductions and perils of popular culture, especially for women. Choosing a slightly outmoded celebrity era, as she did when posing as Lucy, and would continue to do for her breakthrough *Untitled Film Stills*, may have made it easier to stage pictures that offer a commentary on those seductions and perils, and not simply an imitative personification of stardom (her persuasiveness as Lucy notwithstanding).

The 2016 series goes back in time as well, but it seems to request viewers to wear bifocals: We are looking at women born around 1900, and presumably in their sixties at the time of these poses; and we are looking at Sherman, newly in her sixties, gazing on past fame from the vantage of her own middle age. If the young Cindy Sherman seemed most confident in her ability to transform her "self" and thereby to disappear, the face she has presented publicly in much recent work is of a woman confident not only of, but also in, her mortality.

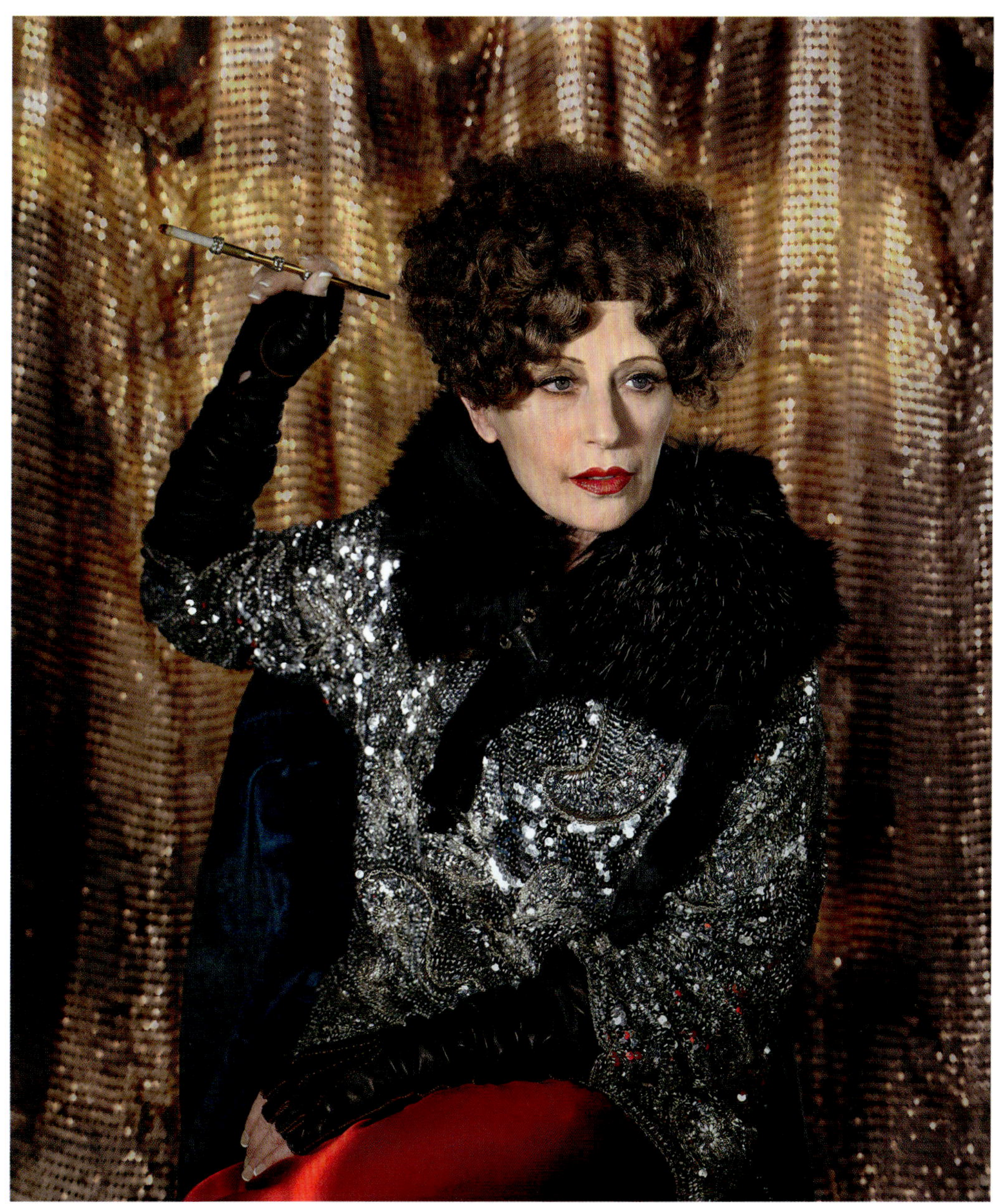

25
Untitled #580
2016
Dye sublimation metal print
108 × 88.9 cm (42½ × 35 in.)
Collection of Richard and Ellen Sandor

Bill Traylor

Born Benton, AL, c. 1853; died Montgomery, 1949

The trajectory of Bill Traylor's career in art tracks that of William Edmondson, with whom Traylor has been matched on more than one occasion.[1] The two men, both Black Southerners of modest means, took up art late in life in the 1930s and quickly came to the attention of leadership at the Museum of Modern Art in New York. They each continued to work prodigiously for another decade or more—Traylor making pencil drawings in Montgomery, Alabama; Edmondson carving stone sculptures in Nashville, Tennessee—but died in relative neglect. A renewed focus on Traylor and Edmondson arrived much later, around 1980, as part of increasingly broad art-world attention to the work of so-called outsider makers.

Traylor and his drawings have benefited in particular from numerous studies, foremost among them a landmark book by art historian Leslie Umberger.[2] Rather than summarizing Umberger's meticulous research, it seems useful here to focus on another element connecting Traylor and Edmondson that clarifies how the two men set about constructing their artistic selves: outdoor studios. As curator Josef Helfenstein observed in an exhibition at the Menil Collection that paired the two artists, "neither Traylor nor Edmondson worked in an isolated studio but in an open, and in Traylor's case entirely public, space, exposed to their communities."[3] Having moved into Montgomery from a plantation outside the city in 1927 or 1928, at the age of about sixty-five, Traylor found himself some ten years later bunking among the caskets in a funeral parlor. It was not a place to spend the daytime hours, and no doubt even more difficult to endure at night. So Traylor moved outdoors. Just as Edmondson chose to use his front yard as a showroom and studio, Traylor decided to begin drawing while seated in between storefronts on a nearby sidewalk. This move greatly increased the chance of encountering interested onlookers from the white art world—encounters that would lead the two men to city-wide and ultimately national recognition.

Just as with Edmondson, however, that interest and those encounters did not seem fundamentally to matter to Traylor. When Charles Shannon, who became a dedicated patron of Traylor and came to own and preserve one thousand of his drawings, mounted a show at a Montgomery cultural center called New South that he had helped found, he took note of Traylor's appraisal: "He studied each picture carefully and chuckled as he pointed with his cane to the many things that amused him. But it was as if he had not drawn them—in no way did he acknowledge his authorship and after that day he never referred to his exhibition again."[4] Much has been made of Traylor's diligent and rapid self-improvement in art, abetted by Shannon and other members of the New South collective.[5] Yet while Traylor verifiably worked to perfect in images all that he had to express, he does not seem to have cared to speak in an exhibition hall.

There could be many reasons for such a reaction to one's own solo show, but we can speculate that the space and context of an exhibition seemed alien to Traylor. Umberger chose well the song verses printed on the endpapers to her mammoth study of Traylor's life and work: "Got one mind for white folks to see / 'Nother for what I know is me / He don't know, he don't know my mind."

Several of Shannon's photographs of Traylor at work, by contrast, show the artist engaged with audiences in the Black business district of Montgomery, centered on the area of Monroe Street where he had his sidewalk studio.[6] Shannon observed that unemployed men would sit and talk with Traylor, and one became a frequent companion, teaching Traylor how to write his name. Boys would stop by to watch him draw, even as Traylor evidently sat studying the passersby. Helfenstein has commented on the circularity of this social setting, which Traylor essentially perpetuated and analyzed as a self-sustaining creative institution: "Traylor simultaneously became absorbed in his activity, participated in the community, and created a nucleus for local art."[7]

In the case of the drawing pictured here, *Untitled (Two Figures, Female Figure Pointing)* (pl. 26), one doesn't need to see a sidewalk drawn under the man's boots or the woman's pumps to register that they are exchanging words on the street. The woman, having perhaps been accosted by the top-hatted man's semiautonomous left hand, is giving him a piece of her mind that might in the next instant be reinforced with a parasol thwack. As befits a gentleman, he is at least refraining from a retaliatory gesture with his cane. The antagonists' moves are matched yet opposed, rendered with a colorful yet above all economical canny that would befit a practiced chessboard strategist.

Shannon, seeking to offer Traylor more opportunities to create, brought him fresh pencils and clean paper, which the artist took in hand only after some time had passed. Umberger surmised that Traylor preferred the paper he found to that which he was given, and pointed out that on occasion he incorporated stains or chance materials into his drawings, for example making a virtue of a column of staples on a counter display card by drawing a bird pecking at one of the staples.[8] Helfenstein took the reasoning in a different but related direction when he noted that Traylor effectively recycled materials just as he connected people and caused them to recirculate through his artistic activity: "He created a symbolic identity between his social status and the junk of the consumer society that was to emerge in the aftermath of the Great Depression."[9]

That Traylor could make such a circuit of connections—among various strata of Black Montgomery, between cast-off materials and original, even self-reflexively modern art, and with Shannon's help, between Black and white society—depended absolutely on his choice of the sidewalk as his studio. For Bill Traylor, remaking himself as a creative figure in his late years had everything to do with imagining art as a social practice. In this sense, he made his self expressly with and through others.

26
Untitled (Two Figures, Female Figure Pointing)
1939–42
Graphite and opaque watercolor on brown cardboard
38.2 × 33.3 cm (15 1/16 × 13 1/8 in.)
The Art Institute of Chicago, gift of Richard and Ellen Sandor, 2025.1003

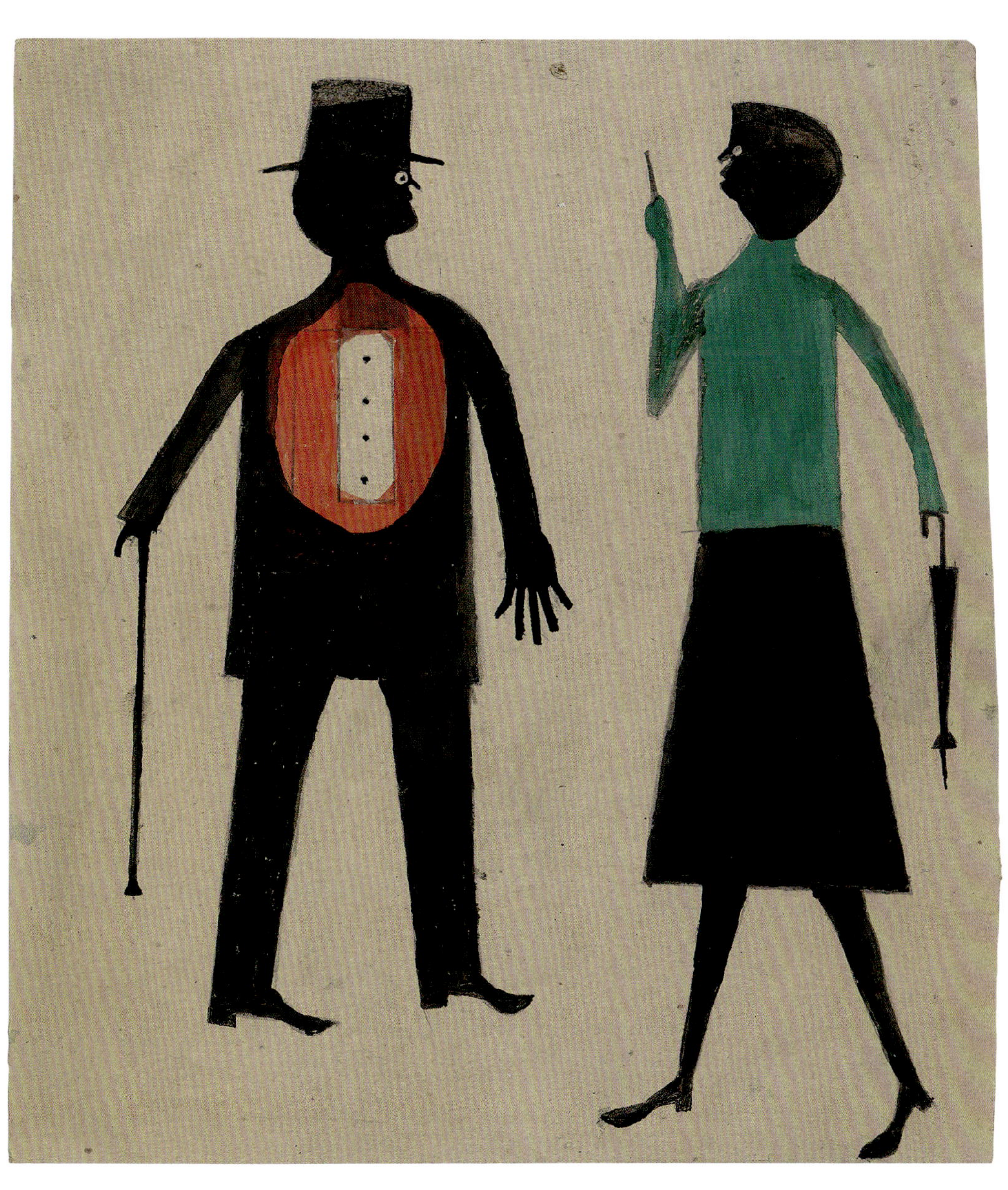

Eugene Von Bruenchenhein

Born Marinette, WI, 1910; died Milwaukee, WI, 1983

The creative self that Eugene Von Bruenchenhein fashioned had many facets—scientific, horticultural, artistic, poetic—all undergirded by a concept of royalty. Von Bruenchenhein, who worked by day in a large Milwaukee bakery, saw himself alternately as a Christlike pauper and a philosopher king obeying the mantra: "Create and be recognized."[1] His single best photograph, a hand-colored self-portrait from 1947 (fig. 1), carries a witty, insightful caption that reads in part: "Edward the First—King of Lesser Lands ... A Fortress of Good." As an additional flourish Von Bruenchenhein adorned his shirt collar with the phrase "Time Produced Non[e] Better." Head cocked above these words, surmounted by a jaunty shock of hand-colored hair that looks dyed as if by a man twenty years older, Von Bruenchenhein emanates the contradictions of a visionary torn between boasting and profound self-doubt.

Von Bruenchenhein—yes, this was his given name—spent his married life in a house that his father built, a cramped storefront erected together with the family residence. As a younger man he joined the Milwaukee Cactus Club and cultivated exotic plants in a greenhouse in the backyard of the same property. From the late 1930s he filled the modest residence with floral hangings or murals; tabletop thrones assembled from leftover chicken bones; head-size crowns made from clay that he had salvaged from construction sites; end-of-days conflagrations painted with his fingertips or brushes made of straws and filled with his wife's hair; and Blakean poems or other writings. His house was a miniature, cosmic kingdom, lovingly tended by a pair of monarchs.

Evelyn or Eveline Kalka, who took the name Marie Von Bruenchenhein, enthusiastically filled the incongruously intertwined roles of queen, muse, and matinee idol for her husband. One small wall in their home held a mere handful of the several thousand photographs that they produced together: black-and-white pictures made in the first half of the 1940s, when she was in her twenties, and a run of color slides as well as hand-colored, often larger versions of the earlier prints made one decade later.[2] Many of the pictures show Kalka half-undressed or fully unclothed, so perhaps one or both collaborators considered them unsuitable for display even at home. Although Von Bruenchenhein tried with limited success to place his paintings and sculptures on

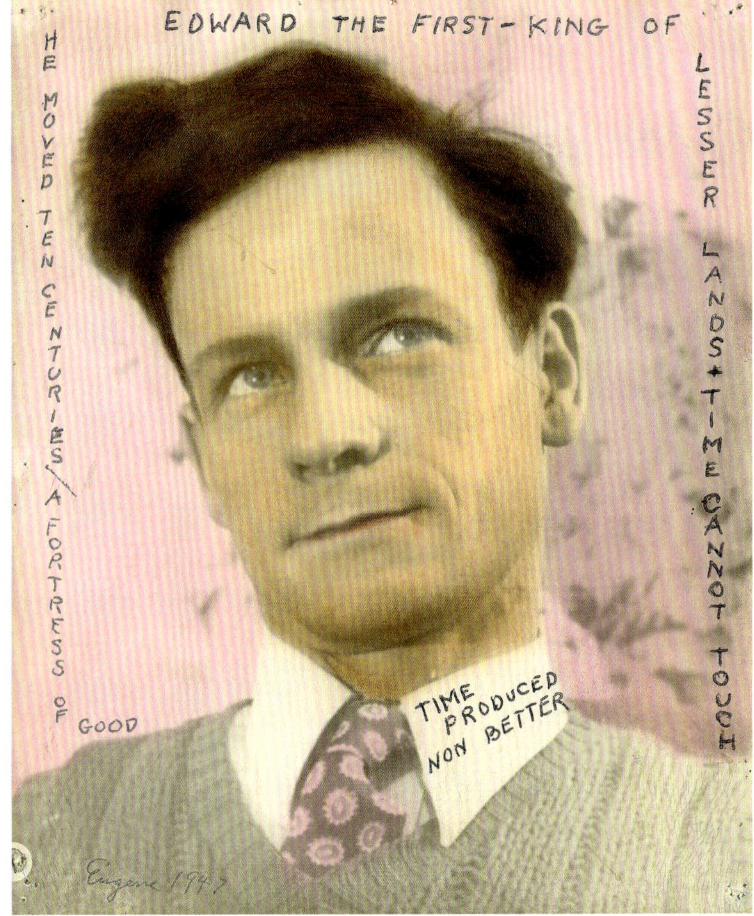

Figure 1 Von Bruenchenhein. *Time Produced Non Better (Self-Portrait)*, 1947. Hand-colored gelatin silver print; 25.1 × 20.3 cm (9 7⁄8 × 8 in.). John Michael Kohler Arts Center Collection.

exhibition, and did manage to publish a couple of his poems, he does not seem to have attempted to secure any public visibility for the photographs, their considerable number notwithstanding.

Curator Joanne Cubbs, who interviewed Kalka shortly after Von Bruenchenhein's death, initially concluded that the photographs were a weak link in the artist's chain of production, a reductive projection of "a not-so-subtle symbol of female sexuality" onto his creative and romantic partner that diminished her into "a figment of Von Bruenchenhein's vivid imagination."[3] In a more recent assessment, Cubbs noted that the artist mixed clippings from girlie magazines with others showing reproductions of classical, Neoclassical, and Romantic works of art, including two paintings by Jean-Auguste-Dominique Ingres—*The Valpinçon Bather* (1808,

Musée du Louvre) and *The Source* (1856, Musée d'Orsay). Cubbs concluded with the pithy observation that "his tireless fetishizing of Marie's youth and beauty [yields] a peculiar hybrid of art and erotica and ... the unlikely union of Bettie Page and Botticelli."[4] The mixture of aesthetic registers is in fact striking, and not necessarily less successful as "camp," really, than the cited works by Ingres himself, or perhaps Cubbs's choice of a Florentine Renaissance model.

Whether at Von Bruenchenhein's direction or through her own suggestions, Kalka consistently conjoined sexuality to innocence or even chastity. On the evidence of the published photographs, it seems that she never followed Bettie Page's examples of athleticism, coyness, or vamping (not to mention that Page's pinup career stretched principally from 1950 to 1957, so many of the Von Bruenchenheins' photographs likely preceded them). In the seven pictures reproduced here, Marie poses with beatitude, eyes trained heavenward or toward an imagined, white-horsed savior. It's a timid, or fetchingly awkward, synthesis; one image that could suggest sexual satisfaction, which shows Marie reclining (pl. 31), could equally represent an instance of angelic rapture. When her full body is on display, as in the three views of Marie posed in front of floral drapery (pls. 28–30), Kalka metaphorically clothes the nudity of men's magazines in tableaux lifted from paintings by Ingres or, perhaps more convincingly, Neoclassical French painter William-Adolphe Bouguereau.

The photographs are by far Von Bruenchenhein's most extensive creative undertaking, measured both by quantity and in terms of the number of years he and his wife spent making them. Moreover, in an oeuvre characterized by inventive frugality (chicken bones, salvaged clay, homemade paintbrushes), this is one body of work whose materials he presumably could not source for free. For these reasons they deserve serious consideration alongside the paintings, sculptures, poems, and other ventures through which Von Bruenchenhein sought recognition as a fine artist. No matter that in the 1940s and 1950s in the United States there was scant acceptance of photographs as fine art, and that, likely for personal reasons, Von Bruenchenhein kept these works from the public eye, and even from the walls of his home.

The photographs of Kalka show the model inhabitant of Von Bruenchenhein's aesthetic arcadia: youthful, desirable yet innocent, and a naturally fecund and prolific being. Above all, she is innately royal: a queen (and her king) without need of subjects other than themselves.

27
Untitled
1940s–50s
Gelatin silver print with applied letters
29.9 × 24.8 cm (11¾ × 9¾ in.)
The Art Institute of Chicago, gift of Richard and Ellen Sandor, 2025.881

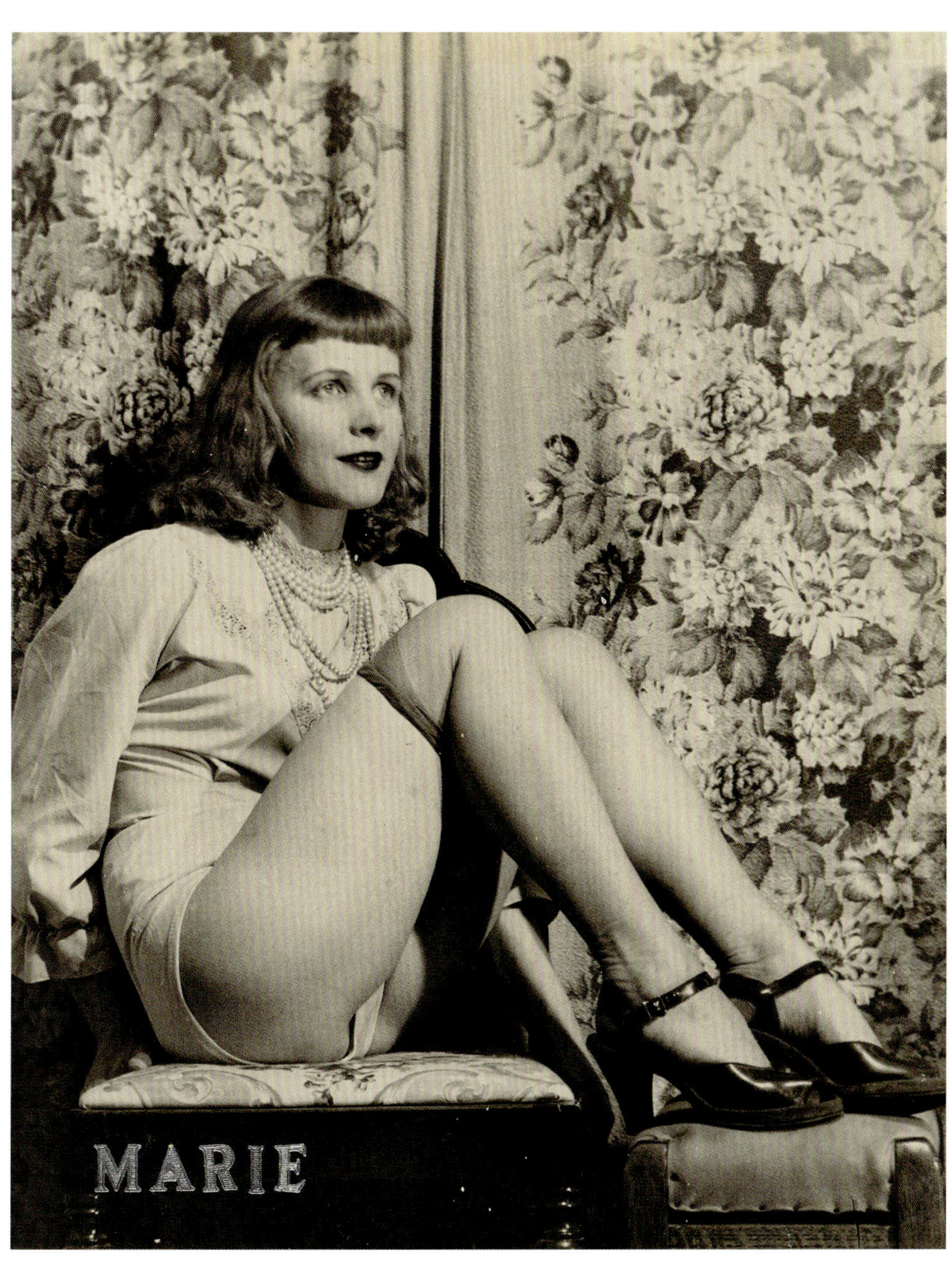

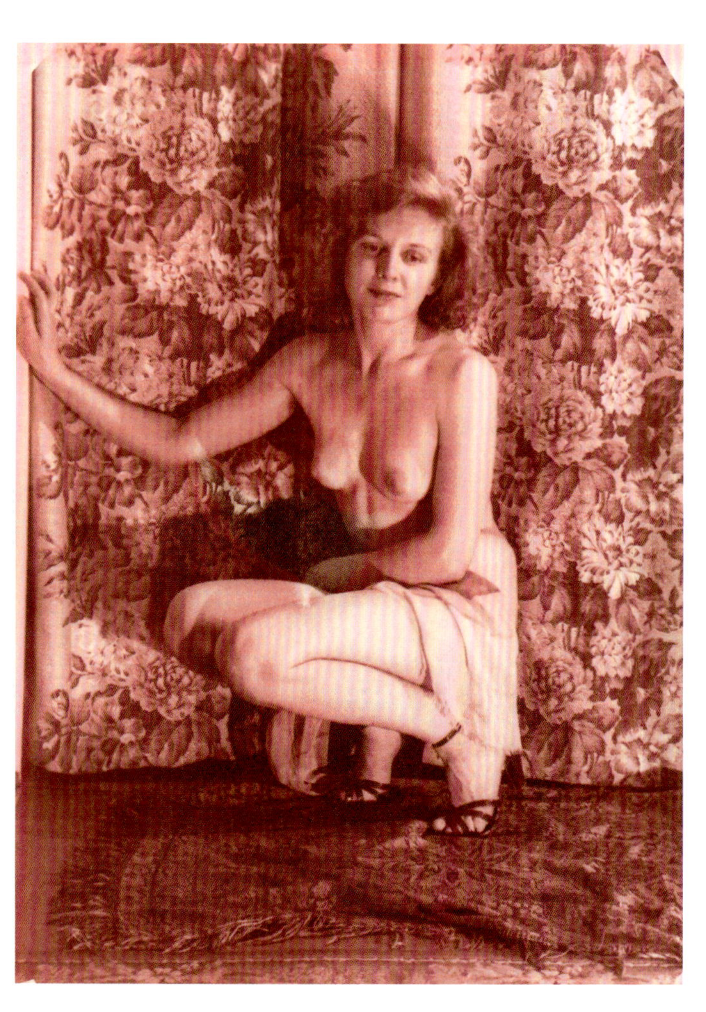

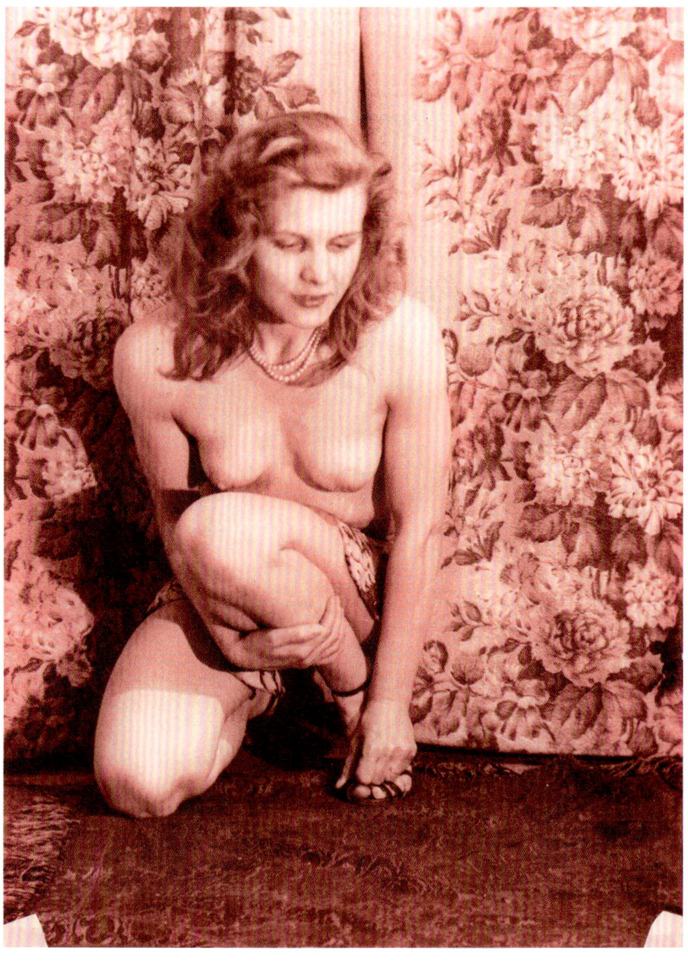

28
Untitled
1940s–50s
Gelatin silver print
12.7 × 17.8 cm (5 × 7 in.)
The Art Institute of Chicago, gift of Richard and Ellen Sandor, 2025.882

29
Untitled
1940s–50s
Gelatin silver print
12.7 × 17.8 cm (5 × 7 in.)
The Art Institute of Chicago, gift of Richard and Ellen Sandor, 2025.884

30
Untitled
1940s–50s
Gelatin silver print
12.7 × 17.8 cm (5 × 7 in.)
The Art Institute of Chicago, gift of Richard and Ellen Sandor, 2025.883

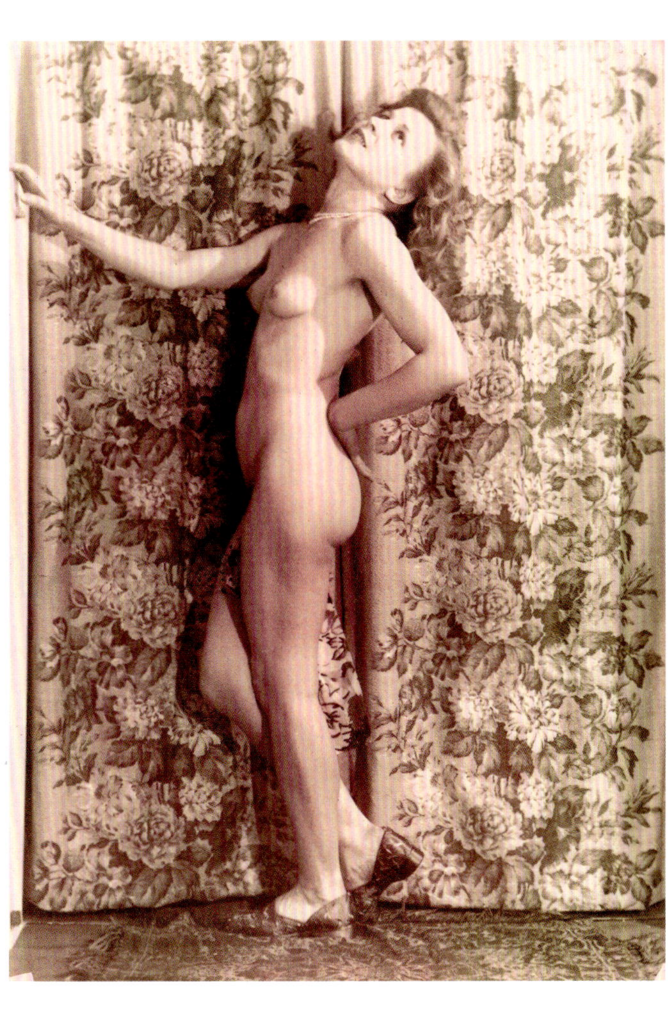

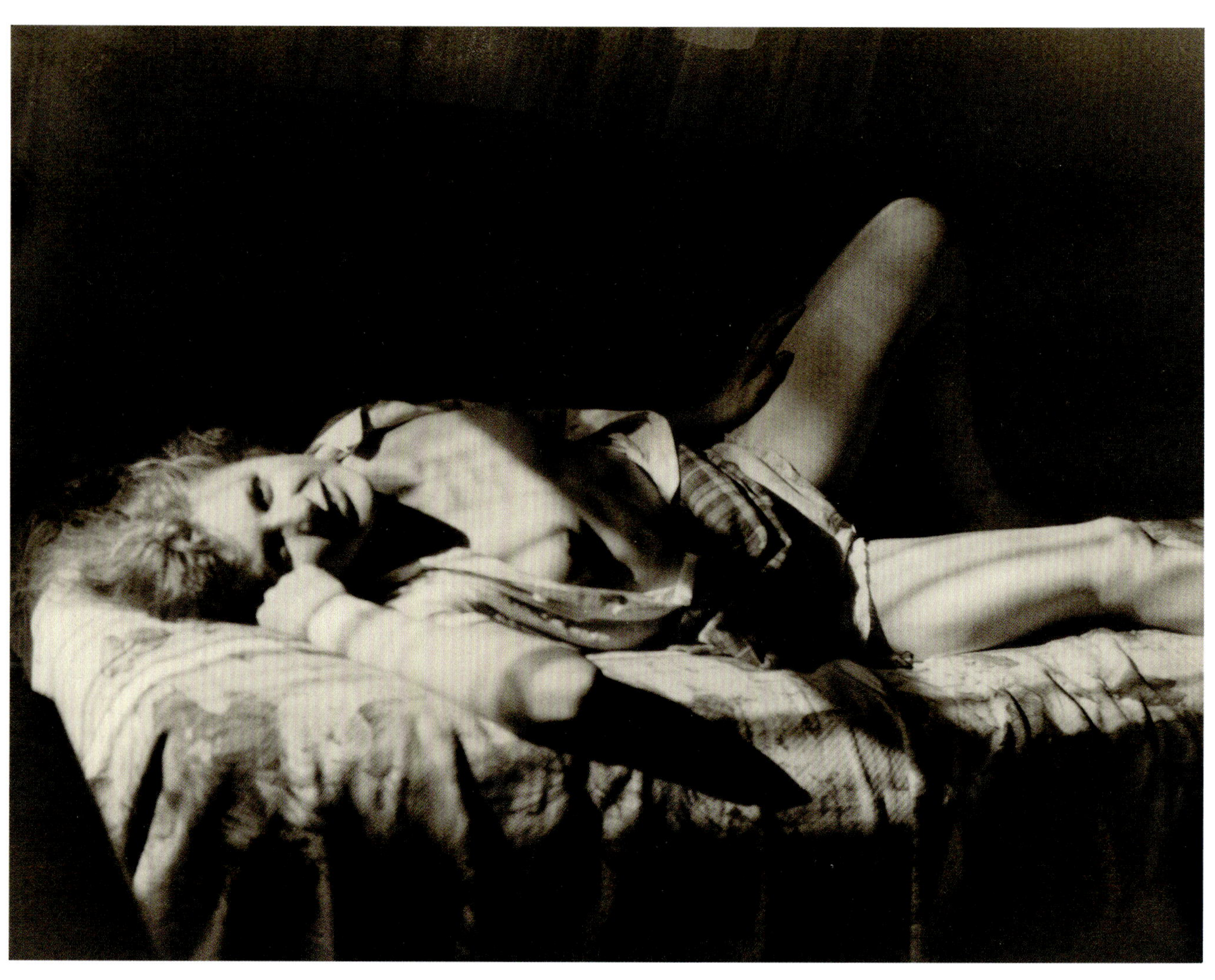

31
Untitled
1940s–50s
Gelatin silver print
20.4 × 25.4 cm (8 × 10 in.)
The Art Institute of Chicago, gift of Richard and Ellen Sandor, 2025.879

32
Untitled
1940s–50s
Gelatin silver print
25.4 × 20.4 cm (10 × 8 in.)
The Art Institute of Chicago, gift of Richard and Ellen Sandor, 2025.880

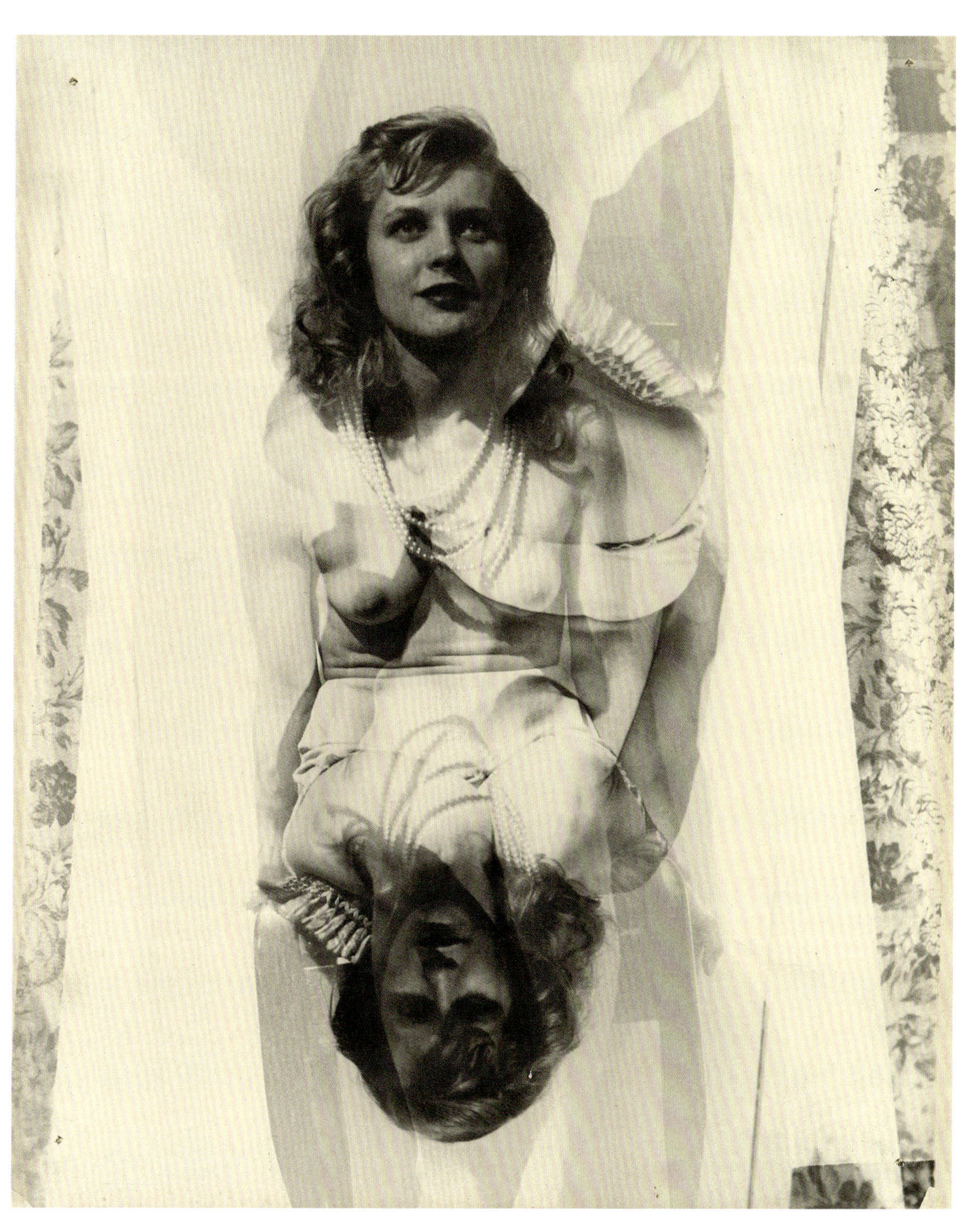

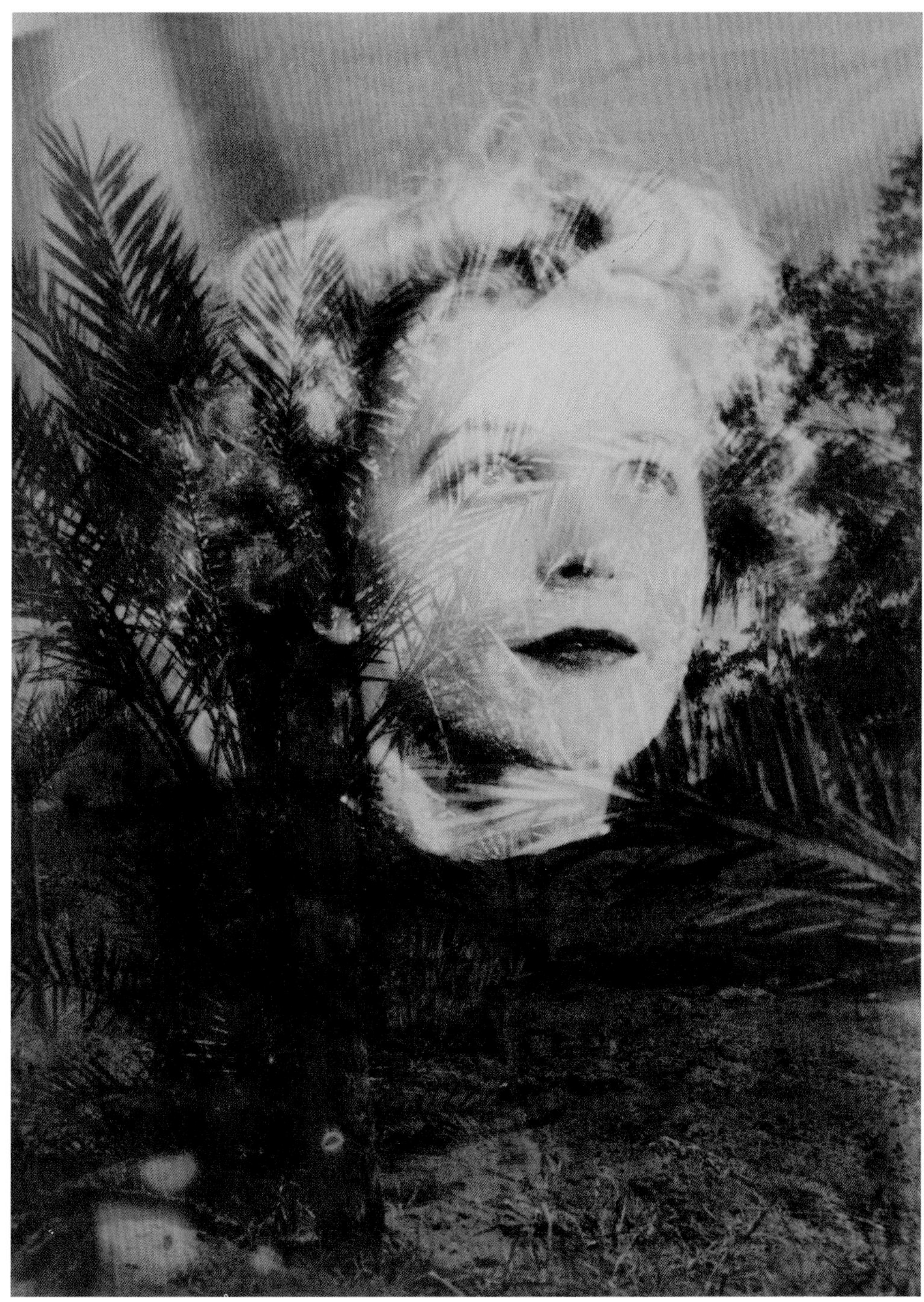

33
Untitled
1940s–50s
Gelatin silver print
25.1 × 17.8 cm (9 7⁄8 × 7 in.)
The Art Institute of Chicago, gift of Richard and Ellen Sandor, 2025.885

Kara Walker

Born Stockton, CA, 1969; active New York

Kara Walker has long been recognized as an artist who cross-wires genres and formats in American culture to articulate the stakes of race and gender identifications in this country. For example, scholars have extensively analyzed Walker's use of revisionist slave narratives, such as *Beloved* (1987) by Toni Morrison, as well as the artist's emphatic attraction to historical romance novels such as Barbara Ferry Johnson's *The Heirs of Love* (1980).[1] More recently, in 2018, Walker figured among the "vanguard" contingent in the omnibus traveling exhibition *Outliers and American Vanguard Art*, categorized as an artist "inspired by vernacular culture" who uses the inspiration to "determine difference differently."[2]

Free, Black, and Passive Aggressive (pl. 34) is, to pun on that exhibition title, an outlier in Walker's oeuvre, for unlike her silhouette cutouts or drawings, which the artist makes "from scratch," this piece is an assisted readymade that uses vernacular cultural production directly. Walker purchased a group of decorative mirrors at an African market in Providence, Rhode Island, and covered them in linguistic interjections, or in her phrasing, "used them as a springboard for automatic writing."[3] The *Outliers* exhibition made manifest the complex dialogues sustained in the United States among so-called self-taught, folk, and visionary makers and those accredited as fine artists, through schooling and the culture industry. This early work by Walker embodies such a dialogue in its very presence, and furthers the artist's core interest in revisiting and revising American vernacular genres. It is exceptional, however, because of its materials—a found object, a set of mirrors—and, quite significantly, as a product presumably made for and likely by African Americans.

Walker has repurposed found materials at other moments, if infrequently.[4] In 2005 she "annotated"—as she termed it—engraved illustrations from *Harper's Pictorial History of the Civil War*, a popular compendium first published in 1866, to make an editioned print portfolio. Meanwhile, Walker has often employed words both on and around her works, giving extensive titles to individual pieces and to exhibitions; deploying language alongside and on a par with figure drawing; and making drawings composed entirely of painted words.[5]

Free, Black, and Passive Aggressive remains unusual in that the "substrate"—the mirrors, which constitute in fact most of what the piece puts on display—are Afrocentric creations. The parade of lithe female dancers and muscled warriors, pyramids and patterned dresses, and ritual displays of sovereignty and celebration all channel decades of Pan-African tropes intended to generate "positive images of strength [and] bring respect and dignity to human life," according to Paul Collins, an artist named on one of the mirrors.[6] The maker or makers of these mirrors are, like Collins, aiming squarely at a Black consumer market. And Walker, in this instance, turned to that market for inspiration. "I used to spend more time at flea markets looking for historical racist paraphernalia," Walker recalls, "but these [mirrors] struck me as a strangely ineffectual antidote to what I had been searching for."[7]

The unnerving ambivalence that is a hallmark of Walker's work comes through forcefully in this lapidary recollection of the mirrors as "a strangely ineffectual antidote." Standard-issue, recently made Afrocentric consumer goods offer a fairly toothless counter to the historical weight of White racist caricature. Walker would not be one to increase the chances of Afrocentrism winning a Black v. White contest of stereotypical representations—at least not directly—for hers is the language of self-doubt, paranoia, and a vomiting forth of repressed desires. "To add some *meaning* to our con-venien-tly *resolved* lives," she scrawls atop the body of a female dancing figure, clad only in a bikini, leg rings of raffia, and vaguely tribal body markings. (A sausage-like scrim of translucent white on this mirror serves to make Walker's handwriting more legible; it also acts, with acid contradiction, to veil the oversexed figure while flaying the clichés that she represents.)

John Beardsley, a participant in a roundtable exchange published in the *Outliers* catalogue, explained "vernacular culture" as oriented toward domestic life and functional objects: two qualifications well-fitted to these mirrors. Beardsley contrasted this with "more idiosyncratic and imaginative forms" that arise within popular culture, borrowing from mass-market products to offer critical purchase on society and one's place in the world.[8] The mirrors belong to an ethnic vernacular culture that shapes identity but may not spur resistance to the larger forces and histories informing that identity.

The period directly preceding the making of *Free, Black, and Passive Aggressive* was pivotal for Walker, who featured in the

1997 Whitney Biennial and received a MacArthur "genius grant" the same year. The artist may have had occasion to consider anew her artistic motivations, and this work in particular suggests through its title and materials a moment of self-assessment. In early 1997, as well, Walker held a show at the Renaissance Society at the University of Chicago, which was accompanied by a sizable artist's publication. Walker interleaved texts—mostly her own—and images—a mix of found and drawn—to create a kind of nonlinear sourcebook for the art on view in the exhibition. At the center of the book, she placed a page-long typescript from her graduate school days. This draft document from 1992, punctuated by ellipses, cross-outs, and typographic corrections, lucidly addresses the challenges to selfhood for an artist who identifies, through insight, as "free, black, and passive aggressive"—and makes clear that suffering those challenges is a burden shared properly by artist and audience alike. The text reads, in part:

> Inequality is not just a dualistic construct.... It is not just a matter of Black and white, rich and poor, male and female. Contemporary theory concerns itself with the decentering of those commonsense dualities ... exploring the margins of oppression and domination.... My work at the moment takes as its starting ground the *idea* of the Historical Romance [novel].... My role in this novel is so wholeheartedly "other" that I haven't been written in except as the foreign and exotic background ... the dangerous terrain, the dark secret. Either frighteningly sexualized or ignored or ridiculed. The only solution throughout history has been to split into many characters.... The more sustainable solution, of course has been to bond into groups ... around a God, or a theory, or a skin complexion, or a style.... My characters are stereotypes attempting to confront their displacement and hopefully in the process causing the reader of the text (the viewer) to realize the initial placement ... and its location in our collective psyches.

34
Free, Black, and Passive Aggressive
1998
Ink and paint on 16 found objects
Overall: 123.2 × 508 cm (48½ × 200 in.)
The Art Institute of Chicago, gift of Richard and Ellen Sandor, 2025.750a–p

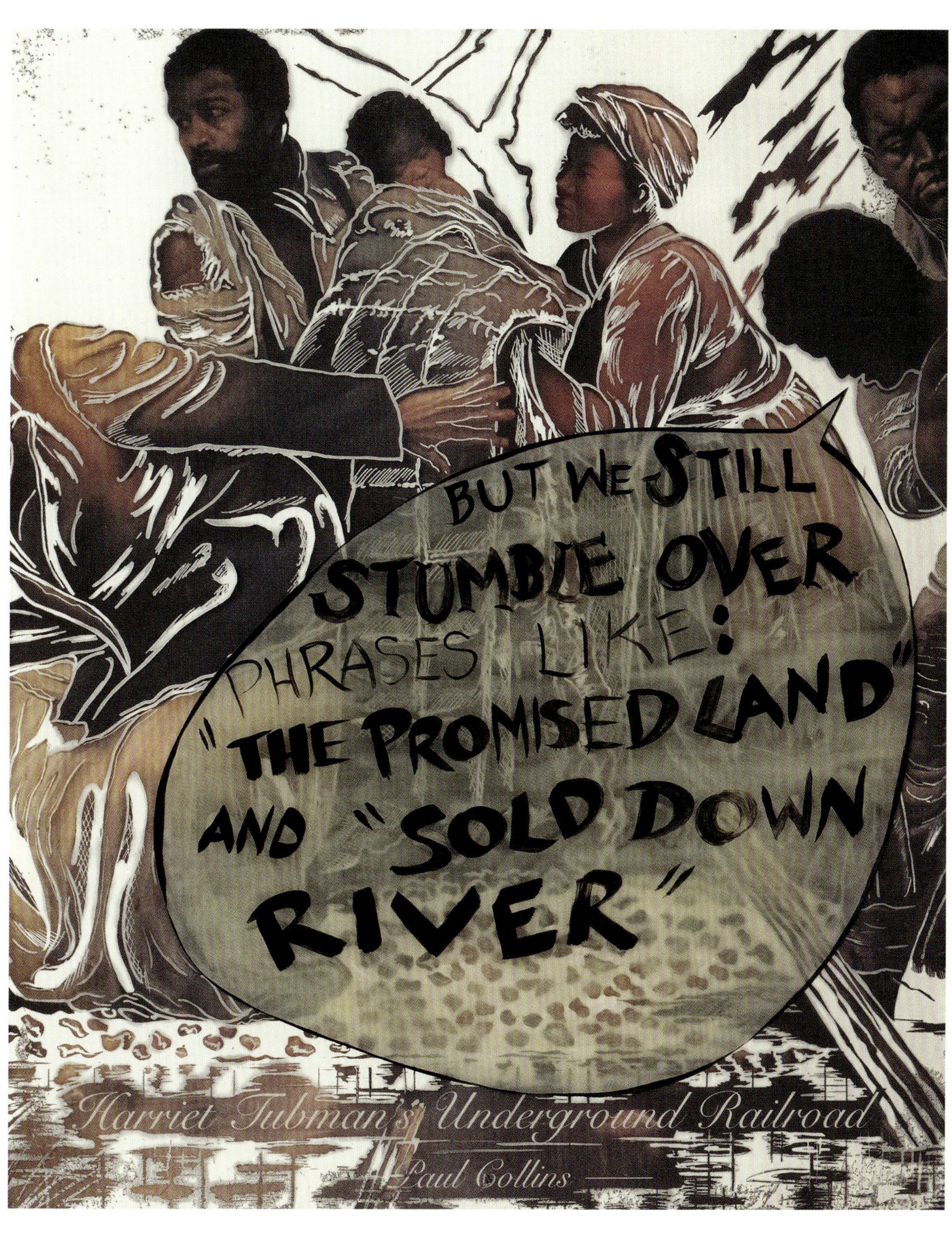

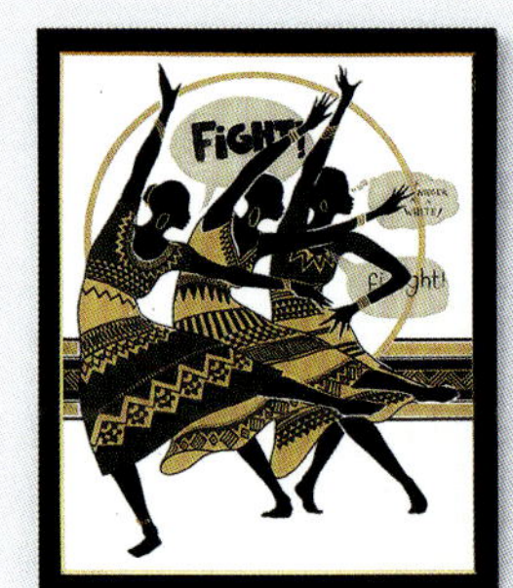

FIGHT!

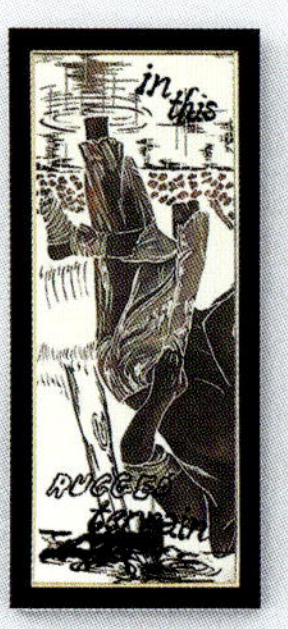

in this

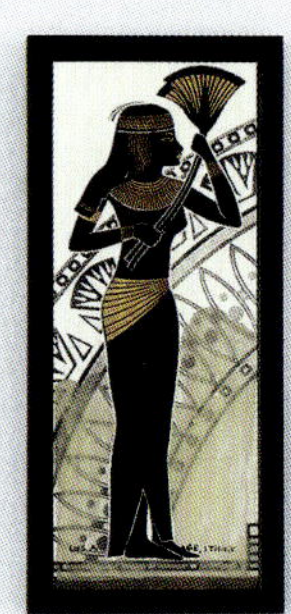
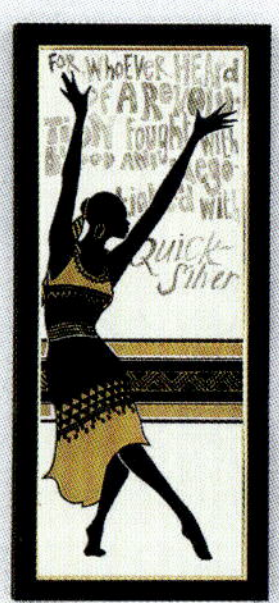

QUICK-
Silver

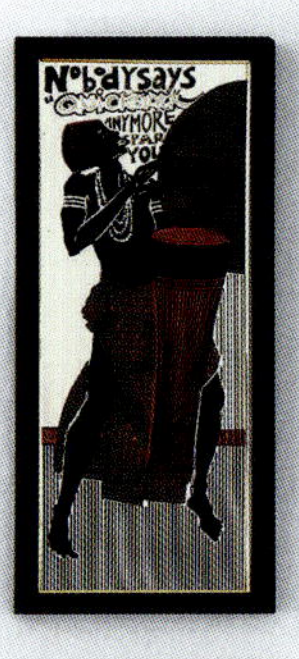
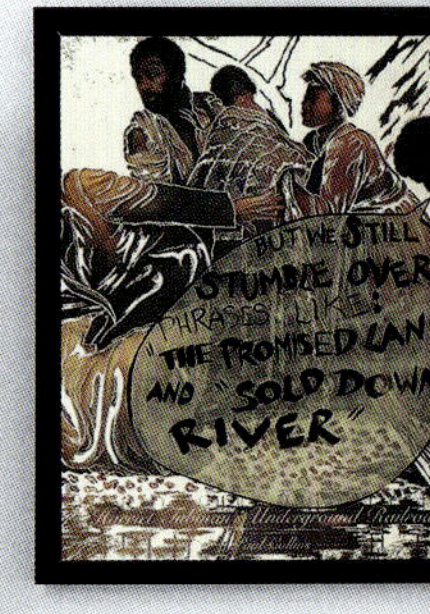

"BUT WE STILL
STUMBLE OVER

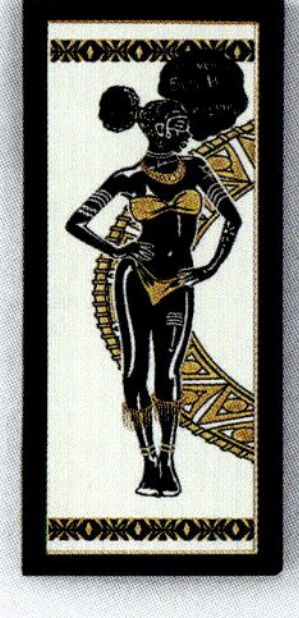
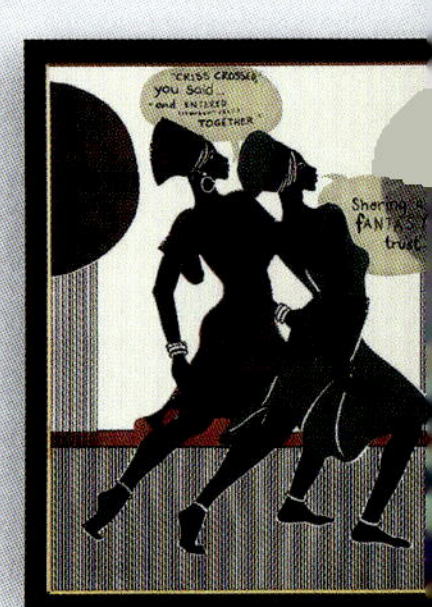

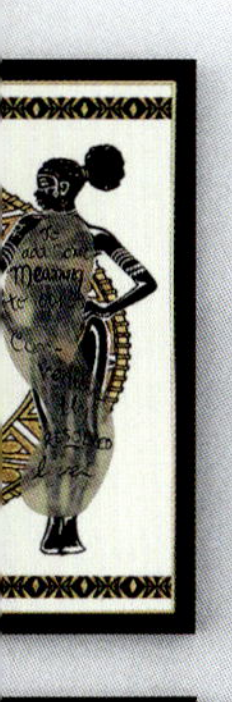
NG-WHAT!?

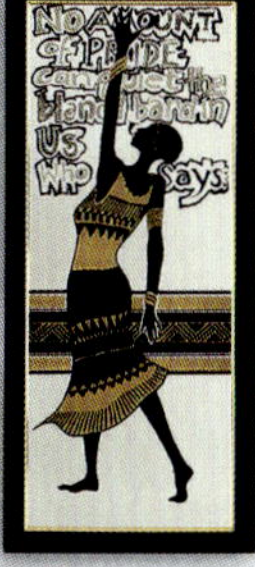
Us
Who says:

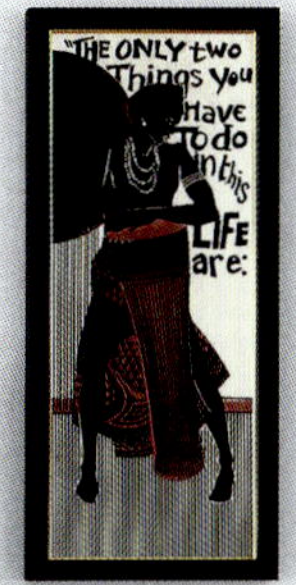
THE ONLY two Things you Have To do in this LIFE are:

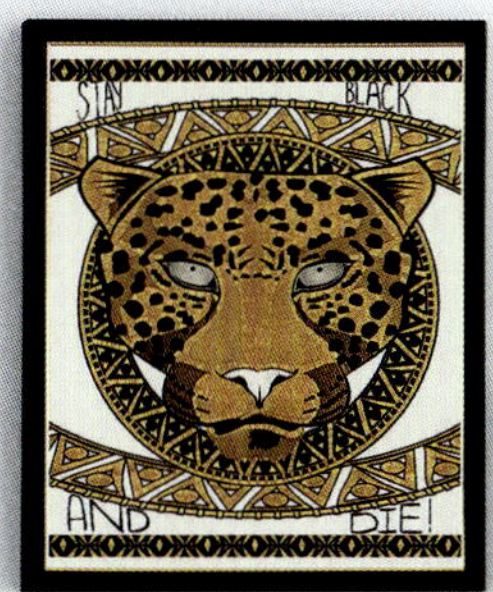
STAY BLACK
AND DIE!

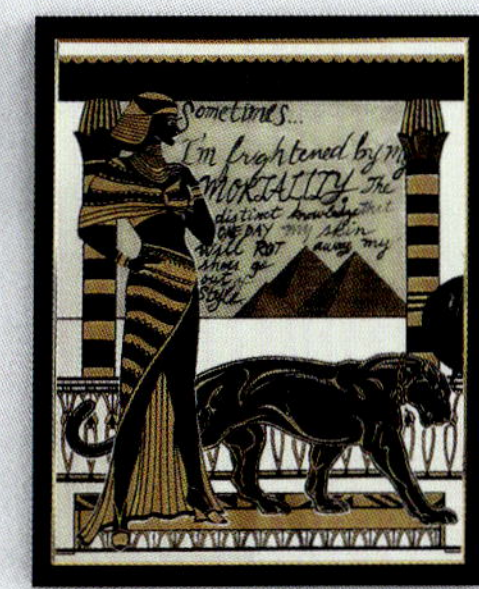
Sometimes...
I'm frightened by my MORTALITY

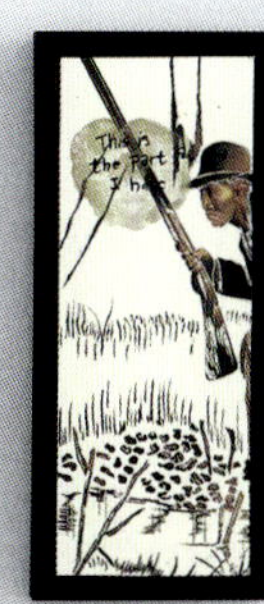

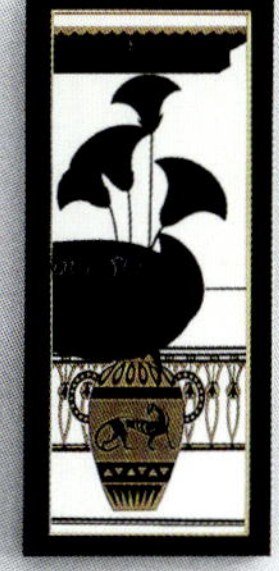

Slim Wasson

Born 1881; died Santa Fe, 1962

Slim Wasson is likely the most elusive "self" in this book. An unsigned obituary in the *Santa Fe New Mexican* offers a rare assessment of his life and career. It credits Arthur "Slim" Wasson with moving "in territorial days" to the Upper Pecos country—directly southeast of Santa Fe—and working as a rodeo performer, then foreman, at Forked Lightning Ranch. The obituary notes that Wasson "was also widely known as a wood carver, a hobby to which he devoted much of his time after his retirement." Most helpfully, the brief vita concludes: "His model of a 20 mule team drawing a borax wagon was a top attraction at the last State Fair."[1]

We may therefore take the magnum opus reproduced in these pages (pl. 35) to be Slim Wasson's capstone as a carver and, one could say, his ideal headstone as well.[2] Wasson joined Forked Lightning Ranch sometime after its purchase and naming by Tex Austin, in 1925. Austin, a tall man with taller tales, had founded a rodeo business a decade earlier and launched Forked Lightning as one of the country's first dude ranches.[3] Austin bought three parcels of land totaling 5,500 acres, centered on a famous trading post along the Santa Fe Trail. He introduced electricity, heating, and plumbing to the property and secured stays from actor Will Rogers, aviator Charles Lindbergh and his wife, Anne Morrow, and other "patriotically minded" celebrities during the Roaring Twenties. A brochure from the time offered as activities: "Riding parties, picnics, a set of tennis, a round of golf, a game of croquet, horseshoes, or ping pong," as well as the use, "day or night" of one horse per guest.[4]

Austin took tremendous financial gambles, a strategy disfavored by the collapse of the national economy. In 1933, seven years after its fabled launch, Forked Lightning Ranch went into receivership, and five years later Austin took his life in his garage. For a few years the ranch fell quiet. Then, in 1941, lawyer and businessman Elijah E. "Buddy" Fogelson,

Figure 1 Slim Wasson on horseback, 1950s. Collection of Pecos National Historical Park, Pecos, NM.

Figure 2 Slim Wasson (front, second from right) and Greer Garson (third from right) at Forked Lightning Ranch, n.d. Collection of Pecos National Historical Park, Pecos, NM.

who had made a fortune in Texan oil, bought the former Austin acreage and more than tripled its size, soon introducing purebred cattle. Fogelson followed Austin's impetuous swagger with a reign of planning and prudence—and he brought far greater wealth to his endeavors. As he moved from success to success, Fogelson found his way to Hollywood, where he met British American actress Greer Garson, the start of a romance that lasted until their deaths. The couple made Forked Lightning Ranch their home for much of each year and entertained there extensively, inviting luminaries of the day such as artist Georgia O'Keeffe, director

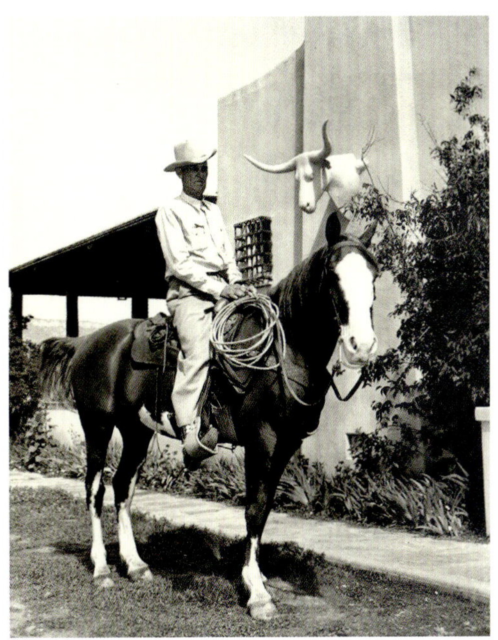

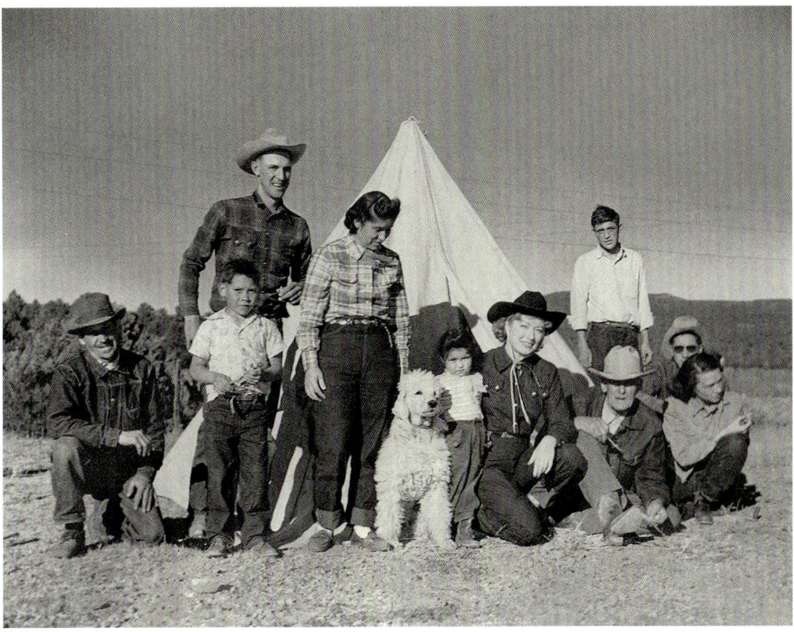

Vincente Minnelli, actress Merle Oberon, and producer David O. Selznick.[5] It seems that Forked Lightning Ranch, in the 1950s and 1960s just as in the 1920s, cemented the standing of Santa Fe as an idyll for coastal cultural elites.

Wasson rode cattle and horses for Tex Austin's rodeos, oversaw their welfare and culling in the Fogelson-Garson era, and carved their likeness in his dotage. Garson—who developed her own enthusiasm for cattle ranching after marrying Fogelson—painted a fond portrait of Wasson in later years, remembering him as a "vintage Marlboro jock" who taught her how to roll cigarettes. He had been given a home on the property but Garson related that he preferred to live in his trailer van, where he "whiled away the hours listening to his guitar-playing buddies" and whittling sculptures out of cottonwood from trees felled by beavers along the nearby river.[6]

"Tall and spare, he was an impressive figure on horseback," Garson recalled. In one casual snapshot (fig. 1), possibly taken alongside Wasson's "retirement home," he sits wedged among the appurtenances that defined his career: property, heads of cattle, and horses. Unsmiling, he appears comfortable on a steed yet tense before the camera lens. In another, a group portrait (fig. 2), he looks reserved and hardbitten—quite unlike the winning Garson directly to his right—fingering a blade of grass in one knobbed hand while resting the other next to an outsized cowboy boot.[7] In both poses he fits the conception of a man who has lived his life entirely on and for the land.

Yet "the land" as Slim Wasson worked it was fraught with nostalgia. A detailed study of the Pecos Valley notes that family ranching in the area had started to decline already in the 1860s, shifting to wage labor in a larger, regional economy. Timber clear-cutting succeeded overgrazing in the 1880s to 1920s, so the land that Tex Austin purchased in 1925 was impoverished relative to what settlers of the preceding century had found.[8] The authors of the study observed that Austin "valued [the landscape] for its scenic, aesthetic qualities far more than its productive capacity"; as for the Fogelson-Garson years, they quoted the estimation of radio personality Art Linkletter, a guest of note at Forked Lightning Ranch: "It was as if a great director had carefully arranged the scene and [Garson] was the cattle queen in some wild Technicolor movie."[9]

The particular commodity commemorated in Wasson's impressive sculpture is borax, or sodium borate. Naturally occurring in dry lake beds worldwide, borax made a sudden leap to commodity status in the late 1800s under a Western prospector named Francis Marion Smith. Smith located and laid claim to new sources of borax in Nevada and California; but just as important, he heavily marketed the memory of the teams of eighteen mules, two horses, and two humans who had plied a competitor's route across the Mojave desert for a handful of years from 1884 to 1888.[10] Smith played up this rugged origin story by trademarking his detergent product 20 Mule Team Borax and promoted it by touring mule teams through California and even to New York City. In doing so he wreathed the brief tenure of Death Valley wagon transport in a glow of restagings that shone right through to the Pasadena Rose Parade in 1999.[11] Today Boron, California, remains home to the state's largest open-pit mine, which is also the largest borax mine in the world.

Already in the rear-view mirror at that time, the borax horse-and-mule teams lay approximately one century in the past when Wasson brought his massive homage, *Twenty Mule Team*, to display at the Eastern New Mexico State Fair, where it won first place in the hobby class. "I think he regarded it as his best piece of work," Garson noted; she and Fogelson later purchased the sculpture. "It is indeed a reminder of the old West, almost as picturesque as Slim himself."

35
Twenty Mule Team
c. 1961
Painted wood, leather, metal wire and hardware, rubber, and cotton
43.2 × 32.1 × 461.1 cm (17 × 12 ⅝ × 181 ½ in.)
The Art Institute of Chicago, gift of Richard and Ellen Sandor, 2025.621

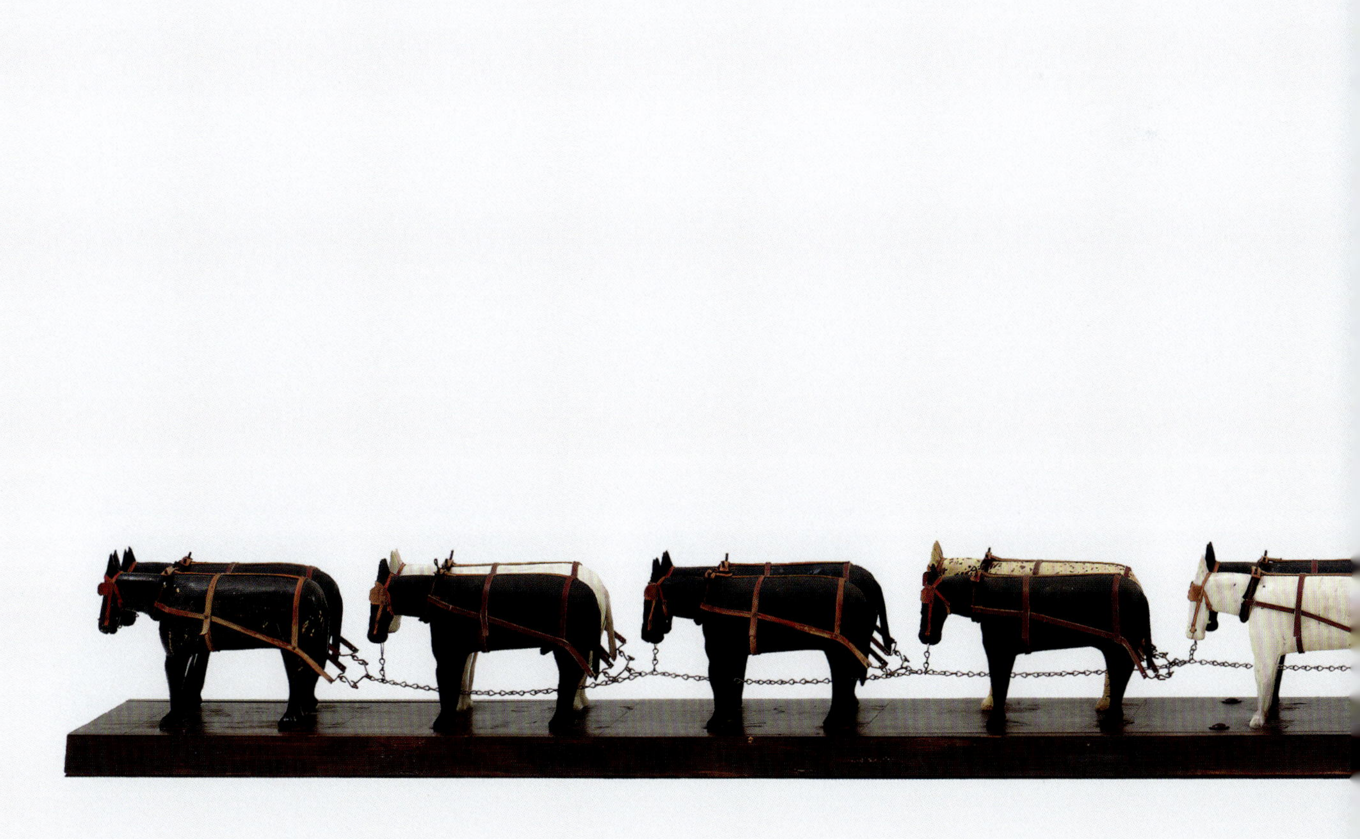

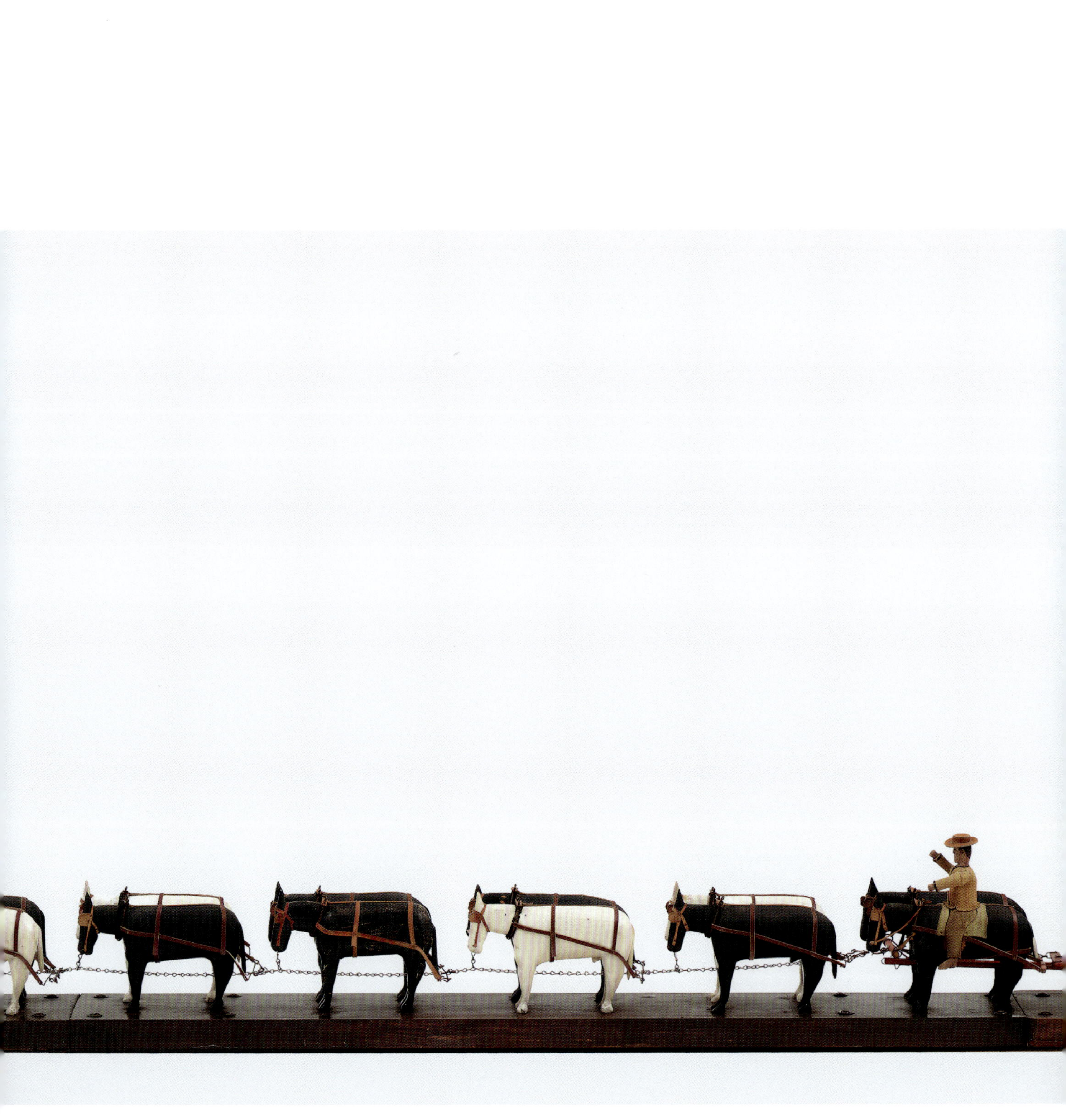

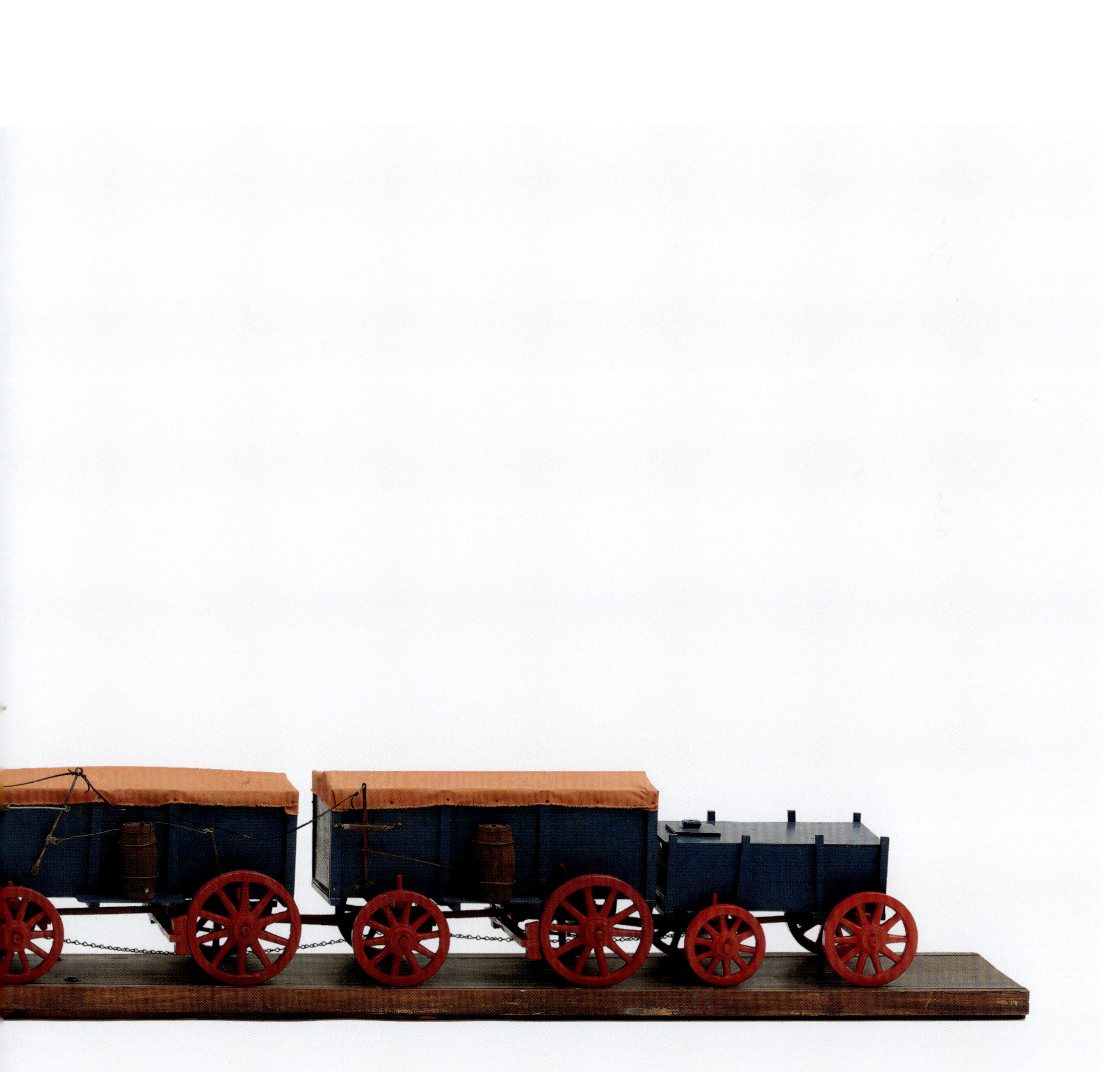

John Waters

Born Baltimore, 1946; active Baltimore

Filmmaker and visual artist John Waters is also a widely published author. At his suggestion, this entry has been compiled from otherwise unpublished press releases that he wrote, in the first or third person, to accompany a series of solo exhibitions held between 1997 and 2011 at the Arthur Roger Gallery in New Orleans.— MW

Five Statements on Self-Making and Collecting
by John Waters

1.
In a series of stills shot from televised movies and his own array of scandalous films, John Waters splices his way through film history to create an outrageous exhibition filled with audacious pairings that serve as an iconoclastic commentary on the great, the glamorous, and the obscure. Waters wants to erase your original perception of these films and replace them with his own self-directed version. (1997)

2.
"For years I took photographic stills from movies. It started with taking shots off a TV monitor. Then I also began photographing other directors' films, because I wanted the 'final cut.' I moved on to do 're-titling' and then even 'double-billing' by juxtaposing photographs from different films. In more recent years I decided to get 'artier' by using upgraded photographic equipment. Combining old footage with outtakes from other movies leads to new narratives; more and more I look for fetishistic details that will give a perfect 'double-feature.' It's an idiosyncratic sensibility; I have a pretty strong grasp of film tradition, but what I know best is quirkiness." (2000)

3.
Waters began producing still photographs in 1992 when someone asked for a film still of Divine in Waters' early film *Multiple Maniacs* (1970). No photograph existed of the precise moment in the film that was requested, so Waters decided to make one himself by sitting in front of his television set with a 35mm camera in hand and photographing video images off of the television screen. Waters says, "I blundered my way into photography the same way I blundered into films." (2002)

4.
"My new work focuses on transformation; I take something unwatchable and edit it into a context where it can be seen. I'd like to teach viewers by ushering them into a more focused, attention-paying, seeing way of watching. 'Unwatchable' is the meanest thing you can say in the movie business. But images that you can't watch in a movie theater—in an art gallery, you don't watch them, you see them." (2006)

5.
"I'm concerned that people don't remember movies; they remember stills that they've seen over and over in books, so I try to photograph things in movies that you are never supposed to see. Really, it's about writing and editing. I think up each of these pieces and then I have to go find the images that make a new narrative which many times is the opposite of or has nothing to do with what the director really began with." (2011)

Top to bottom:

36
Self-Portrait
2000
Chromogenic print
37.5 × 144.1 × 2.5 cm (14 ¾ × 56 ¾ × 1 in.) (framed)
Collection of Richard and Ellen Sandor

37
Sequel
1995
Chromogenic print
18.4 × 213.4 × 2.5 cm (7 ¼ × 84 × 1 in.) (framed)
The Art Institute of Chicago, gift of Richard and Ellen Sandor, 2025.886

38
I, Mary Vivian Pearce
1996
Chromogenic print
24.8 × 243.2 × 2.5 cm (9 ¾ × 95 ¾ × 1 in.) (framed)
Collection of Richard and Ellen Sandor

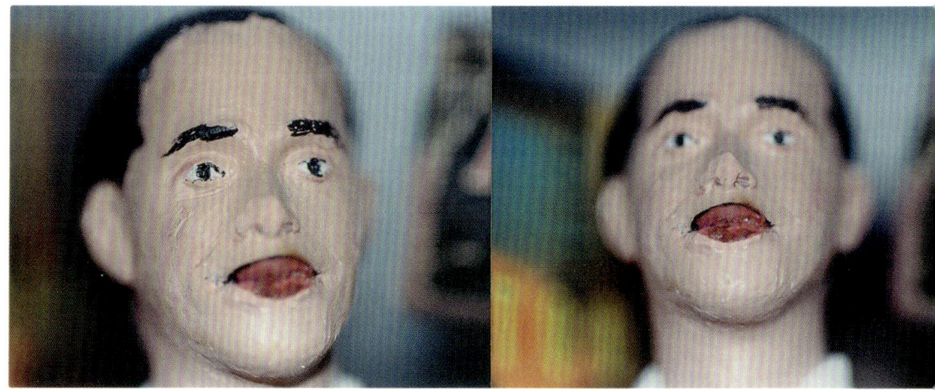

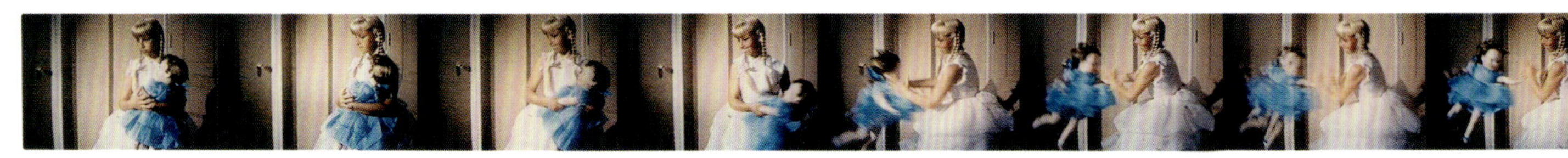

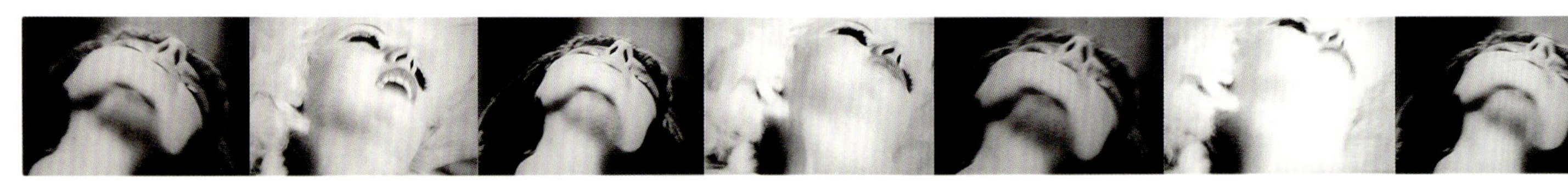

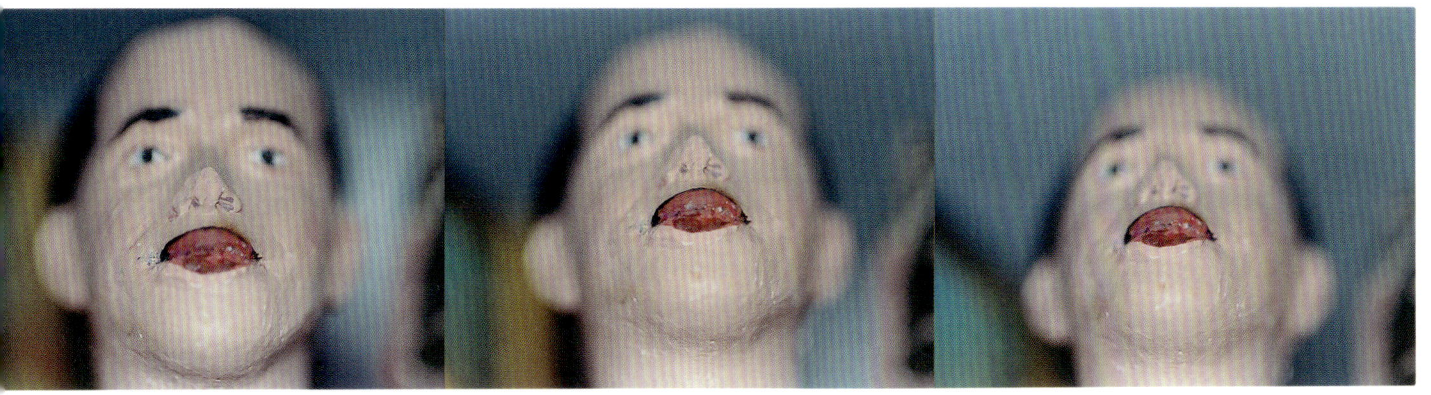

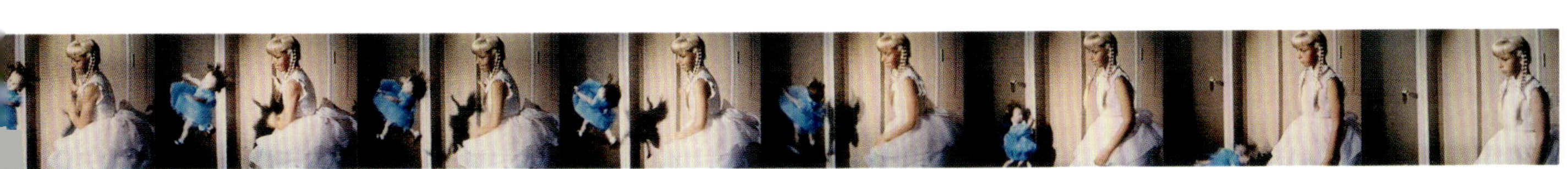

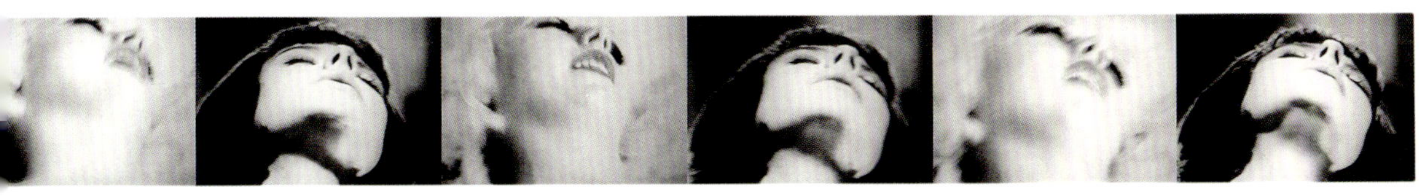

39
Sneaky JFK
2000
Mixed media
41 × 10.2 cm (16 ⅛ × 4 in.)
Collection of Richard and Ellen Sandor

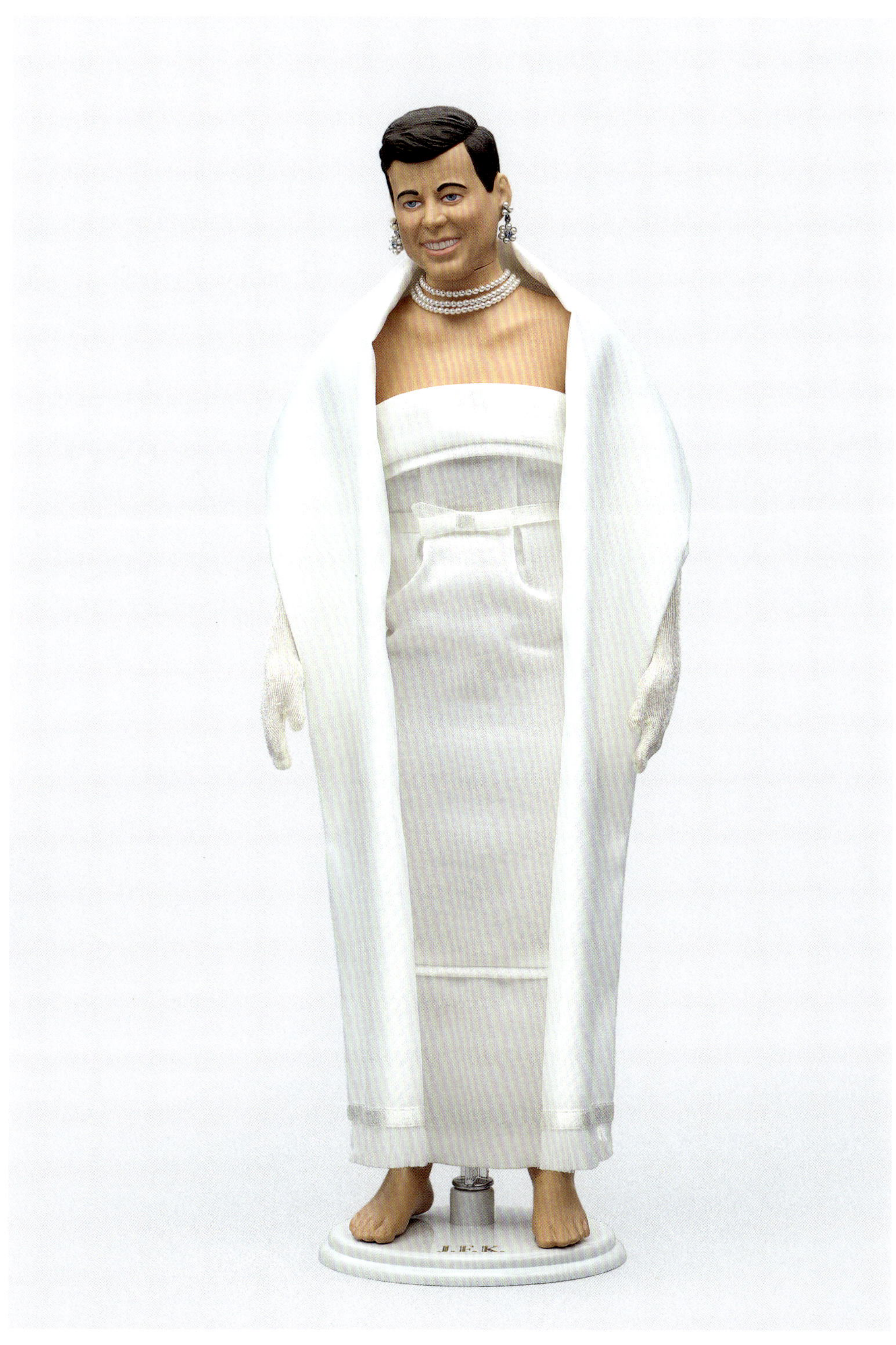

Joseph E. Yoakum

Born Ash Grove, MO, 1891; died Rock Island, IL, 1972

Remember, anyone can dream
And nothing's as bad as it may seem
The little things you haven't got
Could be a lot if you pretend . . .

And if you sing this melody
You'll be pretending just like me
The world is mine, it can be yours, my friend
So why don't you pretend?

—"Pretend," 1952, recorded by Nat King Cole in 1953 and 1961

Thanks to a definitive exhibition and catalogue prepared at the Art Institute of Chicago in 2021, the life and art career of Joseph Elmer Yoakum can be readily assessed in technical, material, art historical, and biographical terms.[1] Like Lee Godie, Yoakum had a lifelong interest in making art that was galvanized in his golden years by a dream, and which Yoakum pursued from then until the end of his life just a decade later. In the span of ten years, Yoakum made about two thousand drawings, many of them captioned with detailed titles referring to mountainous landscapes and natural formations around the world.

Yoakum, also like Godie, encountered a ready audience among students and faculty at the School of the Art Institute of Chicago (SAIC) as well as other Chicago-area practitioners. Artist Jim Nutt bought numerous drawings in 1968, and he and his partner, artist Gladys Nilsson, helped Yoakum secure further sales as well as exhibitions on the West Coast when they relocated there soon afterward. SAIC professors Ray Yoshida and, above all, Whitney Halstead likewise championed Yoakum and his work, which Halstead assessed in expert detail in the 1970s for a planned monograph that the 2021 exhibition finally brought into print.[2]

These fellow practitioners addressed Yoakum with far greater nuance than the artists and collectors who had befriended William Edmondson and Bill Traylor in the 1930s, and even the more contemporary supporters of Eddie Arning and Jesse Howard. Art Institute curator Mark Pascale, who in addition to the Yoakum exhibition has researched and brought forth the work of many in the "Yoakum fan club," has observed that these artists and art instructors explored works from a wide range of geographies and aesthetic contexts "not as so-called primitive objects but as artworks made by artists with a cultural or spiritual imperative."[3] This ecumenical, egalitarian assessment echoes in Nutt and Nilsson's decision to show their own works to either side of Yoakum's in a three-person exhibition held soon after their arrival in California, under the humorous yet ambitious heading *Three Famous Artists*.[4] It reverberates more provocatively, as scholar Lynne Cooke has pointed out, in the title to a 1994 exhibition organized by Nutt to showcase works—including, again, some by Yoakum—that the SAIC circle owned and admired: *Extra Special Stuff: Exciting to Ponder, Difficult to Describe Art from the Accumulations of Four Chicago Imagists*.[5] These artists preferred not to subsume art in generalities, especially not of the kind that place their makers as "other" to conventional markers of creative identity.

Where Yoakum differs from most every artist included in this volume is in his indirect address of selfhood. There are, for example, no known self-portraits in his oeuvre, nor did Yoakum seek to depict his immediate surroundings or even make much space for the city where he lived. The work is certainly grounded in autobiography, or more precisely in the artist's narrativized recollections. Yoakum claimed, verifiably, to have traveled the world as a boy and a young man, and he also purported to have seen every landscape he depicted; this second assertion seems more fabulous than accurate. Halstead, who knew Yoakum well for the last five years of the artist's life, characterized Yoakum's accounts with manifest admiration as vague, confusing, contradictory, and at times fantastical. They mirrored his art: "In acknowledging the nature of the material [I do not intend] an apology for its limitations," Halstead wrote. "On the contrary I am convinced that Yoakum's memories and his colorful tales are an important aspect of the subject."[6]

In this sense Yoakum's drawings and the stories with which he surrounded them coalesce as a reminder that all art is invention and, as such, comes from a "self, made" rather than one that is factual or naturally given. The point is banal—until one considers that the presumption of wherewithal to invent one's (creative) self has not been commonly or consistently accorded to artists of color, women, Indigenous, or queer creators; makers living outside metropolitan centers or in cultures not conventionally connected to industrial modernity; individuals who take up materials or methods deemed lesser or "merely" popular; as well as those who appear uneducated, or "not in their right mind." That is, to put it mildly, a lot of selves.

Yoakum's late work *The Mounds of Pleasure on J.A. Brimms Farm near Walnut Grove Missouri* (pl. 40), for example, carries a reference to Walnut Grove, Missouri, where Yoakum lived until the age of about ten, and again after the age of eighteen—having traveled the world with various circuses in the intervening eight years. (Yoakum's life decisions attest repeatedly to a singular combination of independence and loyalty, wanderlust and attachment to place.) He grew up working on his father's farm yet mentions in a notebook sketch from around the time of this drawing that a "Hdw. And Gas Store Were all This Business There"; it seems that J. A. Brimm owned a hardware store in Walnut Grove, and perhaps Yoakum is conflating two work experiences.[7] Such a move already begins to turn memory into poetry.

Yet it is the description of *pleasure*, a word that Yoakum began using with relative frequency in his late years, that arrests attention and shifts the scene definitively from a recollection of place to a rendering of sensation and deep consciousness. A spindly sun rises to consummate the connection of the pleasure mounds, which might also be heads entwined in a difficult embrace: the one at left with a bank of trees in place of eyes, the one at right caught in a grimace. Yoakum, far more even than Von Bruenchenhein, made Blakean pictures, chaste even in the depiction of earthly matters, and the pleasures in question seem principally to be those of the mind: recollection, ideation, idealization. Yoakum adhered to precepts of the Church of Christ, Scientist, whose founder, Mary Baker Eddy, declared problems of life and the body to be illusions that the mind could heal through prayerful concentration.[8]

Writing about *Nat King Cole Roveing Comedian & Entertainer Age & Birth Place Not Sure* (pl. 42), Halstead called this drawing the equal of a work by Henri Rousseau, citing its compositional tautness and the tension between figuration and pattern: "[It] is an exceptional display of Yoakum's capacity for abstract design..." Nat King Cole's age and place and birth were of course easy to establish, and he was no more peripatetic than any internationally recognized performer of his day. This is not a portrait so much as a projection. Yoakum had idiosyncratic views on Black identity, and perhaps he felt an affinity to Cole on this account. It seems, however, that Yoakum would have identified above all with Cole's mellifluous advice in "Pretend," which contains an invitation to dream and to share the fruits of one's imagination: "The world is mine, it can be yours, my friend / So why don't you pretend?"

40
The Mounds of Pleasure on J.A. Brimms Farm near Walnut Grove Missouri
Mar. 7, 1970
Ink and pastel on white wove paper
39.5 × 30 cm (15 9⁄16 × 11 13⁄16 in.)
The Art Institute of Chicago, gift of Richard and Ellen Sandor, 2025.1008

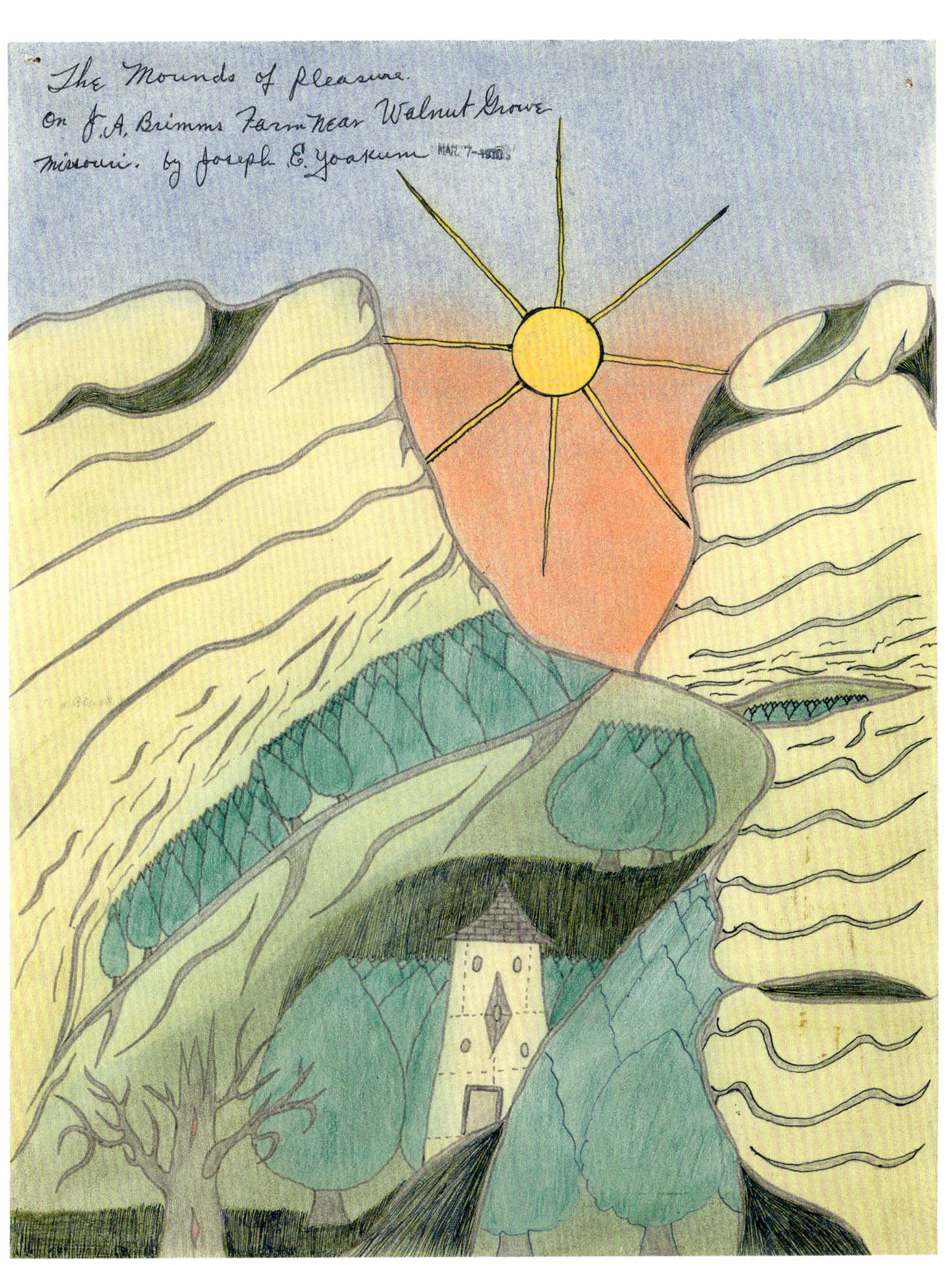

41
Holland Tunnal in Adirondack Mtn Range near Albany New York
n.d.
Ink and pastel on white wove paper
30.3 × 48.4 cm (11 15/16 × 19 1/16 in.)
The Art Institute of Chicago, gift of Richard and Ellen Sandor, 2025.1007

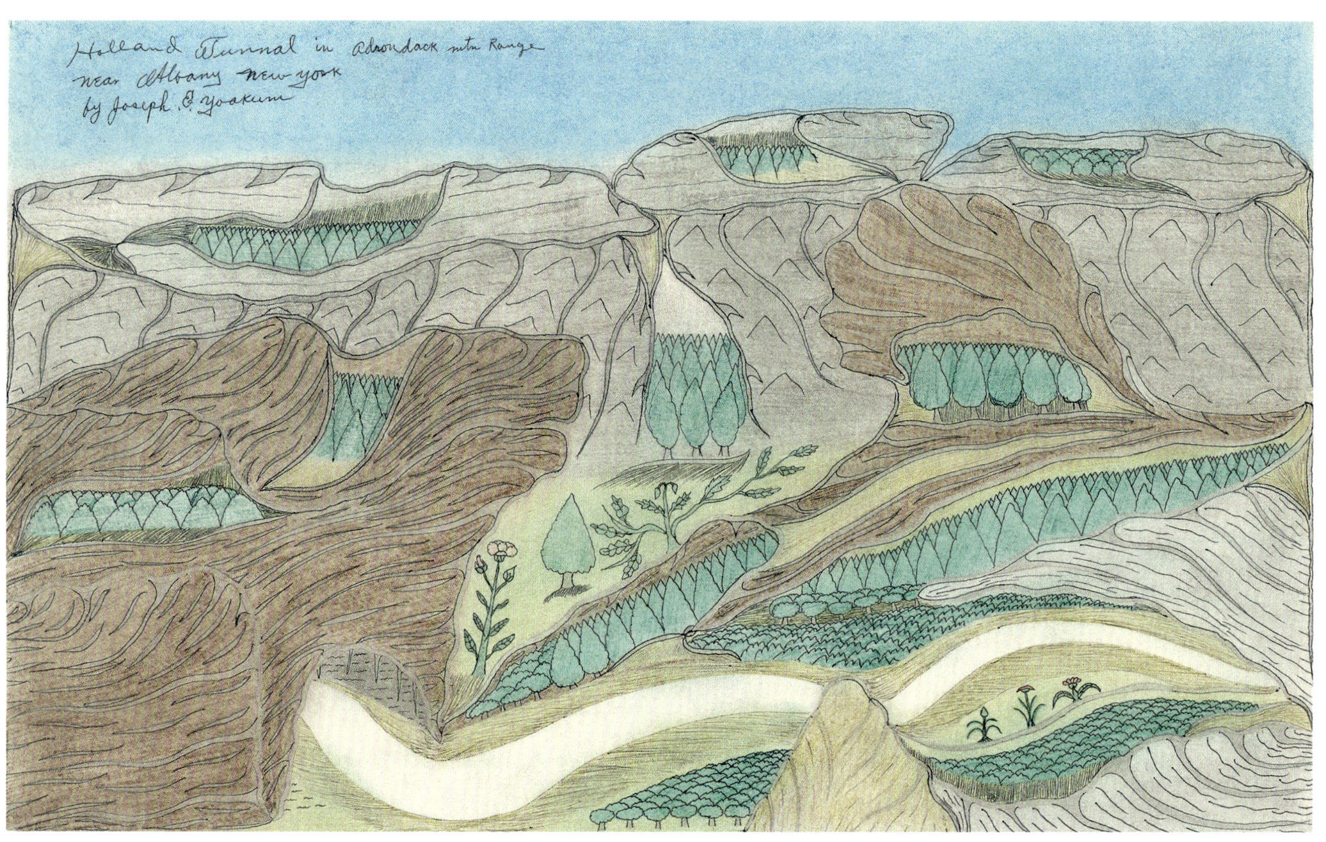

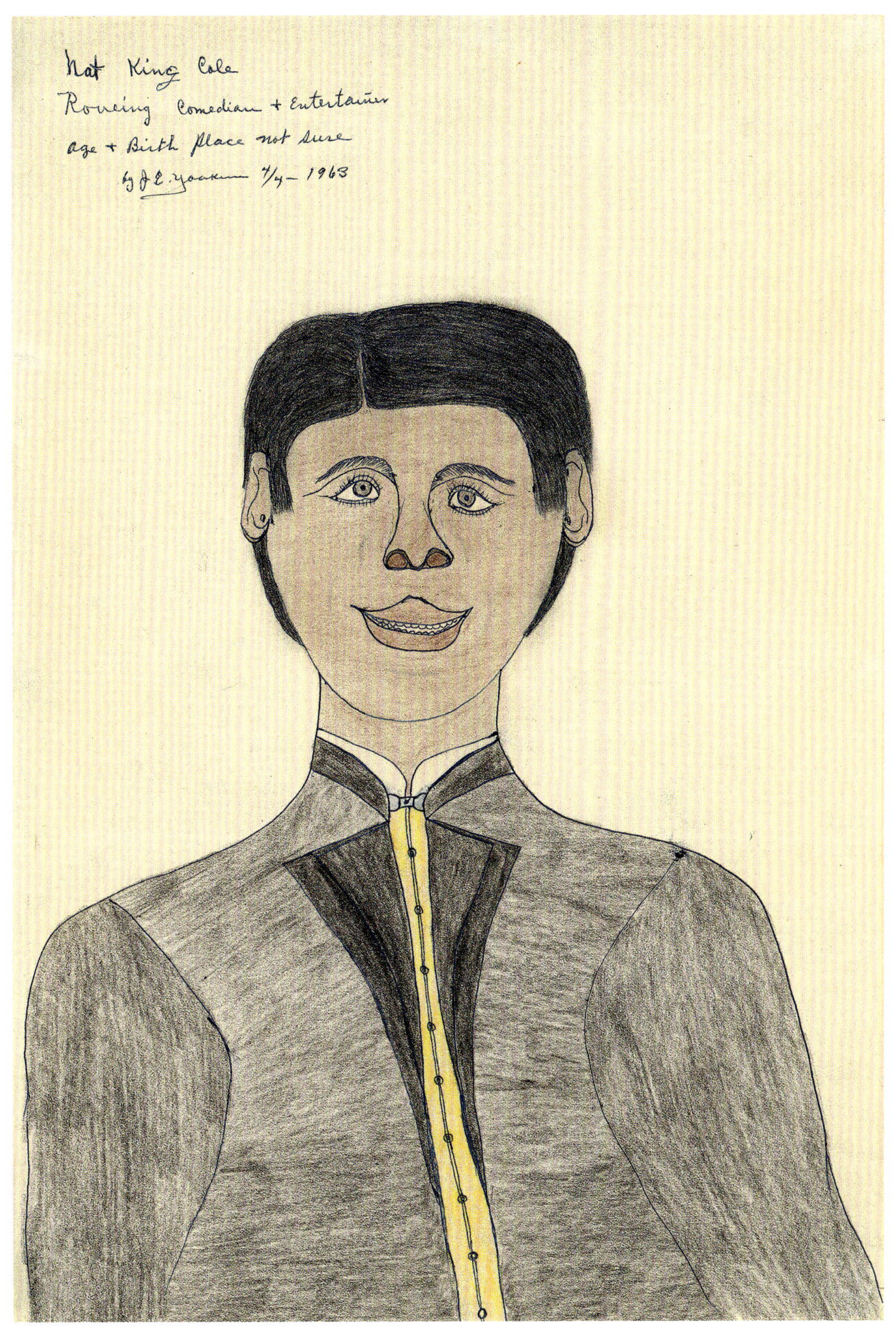

42
Nat King Cole Roveing Comedian & Entertainer Age & Birth Place Not Sure
Apr. 4, 1963
Ink, graphite, and crayon on cream wove paper
45.1 × 30.2 cm (17¾ × 11⅞ in.)
The Art Institute of Chicago, gift of Richard and Ellen Sandor, 2025.1006

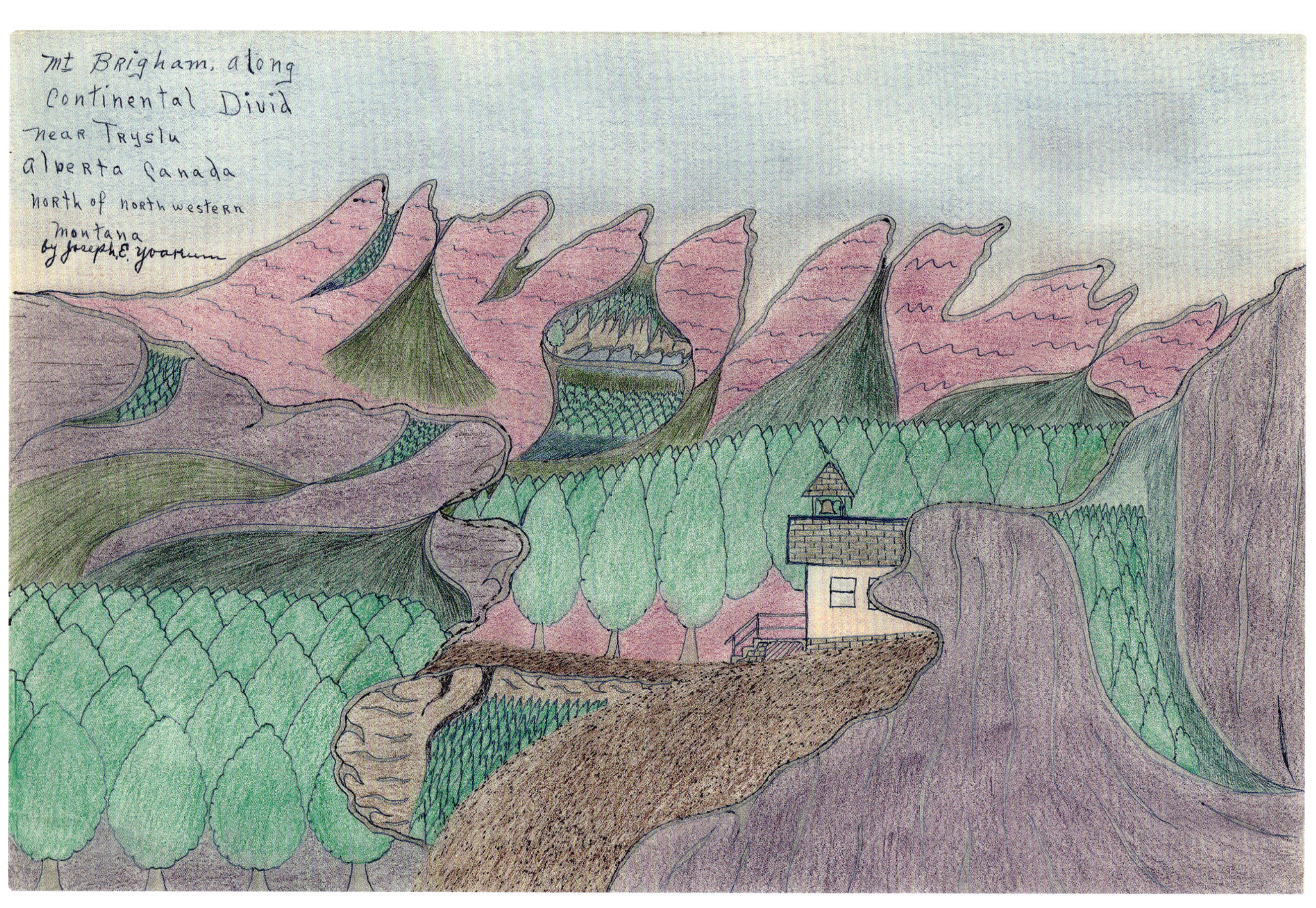

43
Mt. Brigham, Along Continental Divid near Tryslu Alberta Canada North of North Western Montana
n.d.
Ink and pastel on white wove paper
30.5 × 45.8 cm (12 × 18 in.)
The Art Institute of Chicago, gift of Richard and Ellen Sandor, 2025.1004

44
Great Dividing Range of Queensland Sector near Brisbane Australia
June 3, 1963
Ink and pastel on paper
30.5 × 45.8 cm (12 × 18 in.)
The Art Institute of Chicago, gift of Richard and Ellen Sandor, 2025.1005

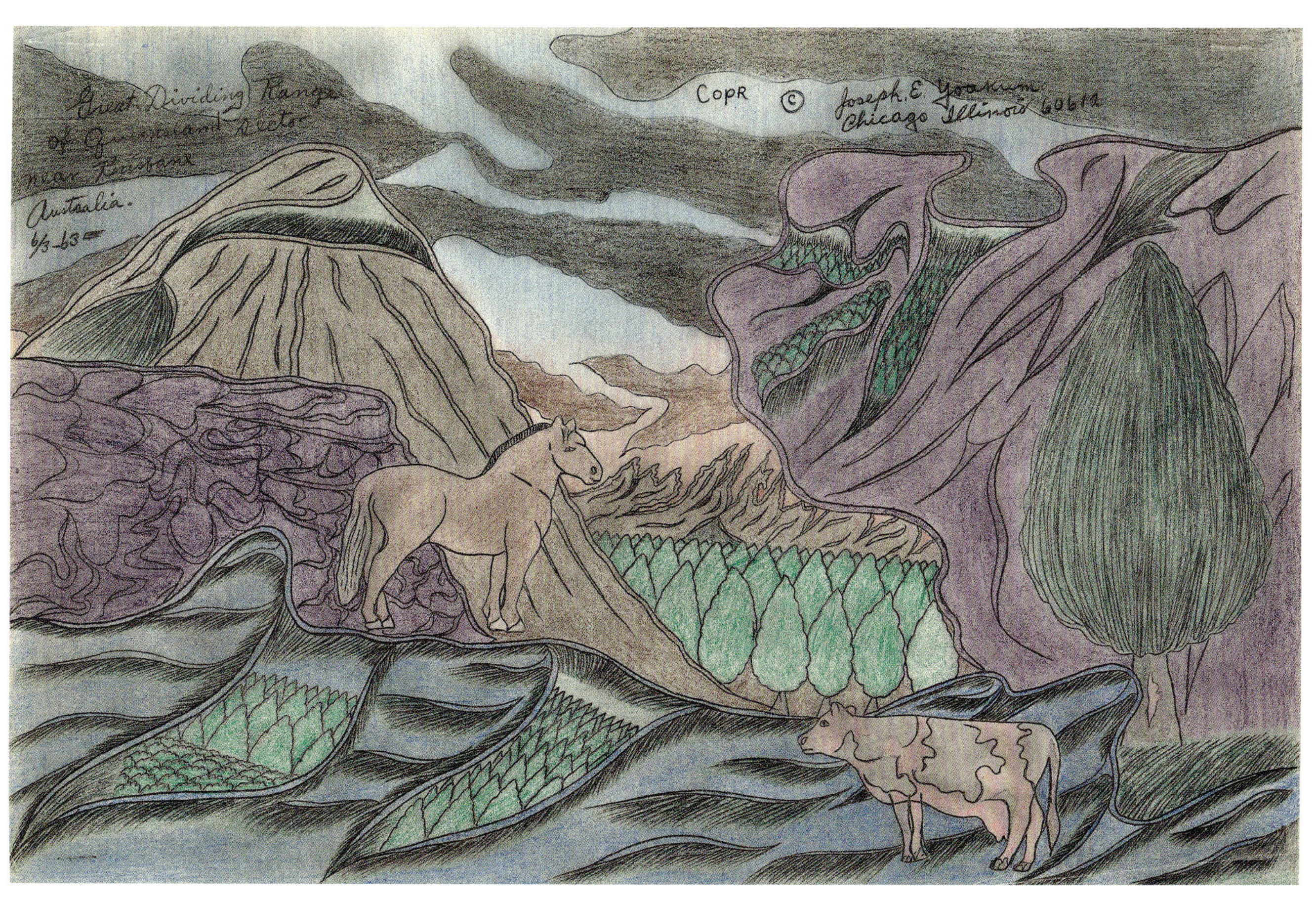

Notes

On Art and Innovation: Richard and Ellen Sandor in Conversation with Matthew S. Witkovsky

1 These inspirations included Fred Smith (born Spirit, WI, 1886; died Phillips, WI, 1976), a sculptor and logger who, in retirement, made more than 200 works in concrete on his 120-acre homestead. The Wisconsin Concrete Park, as Smith called his creation, remains open for public visits today.

2 Sidney Janis, *They Taught Themselves: American Primitive Painters of the 20th Century* (Dial Press, 1942).

3 Intuit Art Museum, founded in 1991 by a collective that included Robert A. Roth and Susann Craig, remains a premier venue in the United States for valorizing the work of "outsider" artists.

4 Richard L. Sandor, "Some Empirical Findings on the Legal Costs of Patenting," *Journal of Business* 45, no. 3 (1972): 375–78. Chester Carlson patented xerography, the process that led to the creation of the Xerox machine, in 1938. William B. McLean led the United States Navy team that developed the Sidewinder air-to-air missile between 1945 and 1954.

5 In May 1969 student activists and allies defended a two-block area recently purchased by the University of California, Berkeley, and named it People's Park. A community association, formed to keep the area open for free speech and antiestablishment activities, still operates today.

6 *E. J. Bellocq: Storyville Portraits*, organized by the Museum of Modern Art, New York, traveled to the Berkeley Art Museum and Pacific Film Archive from March 1 to 14, 1972.

7 While photographs were included in bibliophile auctions beginning in the 1850s, public sales of photographs emerged as a market focus only after the establishment of commercial galleries dedicated to photography in the 1950s and 1960s. Sotheby's initiated a program of regular photography sales in 1971, followed by Christie's in 1972, both at their London houses. In 1975 Sotheby's expanded that program to New York.

8 See, for example, Shawn O'Sullivan, "Collector Closeup: Richard and Ellen Sandor," *B&W: Black and White Magazine for Collectors of Fine Photography*, no. 37 (June 2005): 60.

9 Richard L. Sandor, "Richard Sandor, father of carbon trading on climate change," interview by Emmanuel Daniel, Aug. 20, 2021, https://www.emmanueldaniel.com/richard-sandor-father-of-carbon-trading-on-climate-change.

Artists and Artworks

Eddie Arning

1 The details of Eddie Arning's life and work in this entry are taken entirely from an unpublished doctoral thesis by Pamela Jane Sachant, "The Art and Life of Eddie Arning" (PhD diss., University of Delaware, 2003). Sachant cites just three short writings about Arning published before her study, and nothing monographic seems to have appeared in print since its completion.

2 Cited in Sachant, 108–9.

3 Sachant, 119.

4 Sachant compiled a list of institutions to which Sackton offered as gifts one or more drawings by Arning in the artist's late years. Nearly twenty museums accepted, while more than thirty declined or left Sackton's overtures unanswered (this was the case at the Art Institute of Chicago). See Sachant, 379–80.

William Edmondson

1 Chronology in *The Art of William Edmondson*, ed. Rusty Freeman (University Press of Mississippi, 1999), 212–13.

2 Robert Farris Thompson, "Edmondson's Art," in *The Art of William Edmondson*, 3.

3 San Marino, CA, Huntington Library, *Real American Places: Edward Weston and Leaves of Grass*, Oct. 22, 2016–Mar. 20, 2017, no cat.

4 Charis Wilson Journal and Supporting Material, Huntington Library, box 1, folder 5 (entries Aug. 21–Sept. 12, 1941), cited in Brett Abbott, *In Focus: Edward Weston* (J. Paul Getty Museum, 2005), 84.

5 Cited in Farris Thompson, "Edmondson's Art," 6.

6 Cited in William H. Wiggins Jr., "Jesus has planted the seed of carvin' in me': The Impact of Afro-American Folk Religion on the Limestone Sculpture of William Edmondson," in *William Edmondson: A Retrospective*, ed. Georganne Fletcher, exh. cat. (Tennessee State Museum, 1981), 32.

7 Farris Thompson, "Edmondson's Art," 12, citing in part a 1999 lecture by Mechal Sobel, later incorporated into Sobel, *Teach Me Dreams: The Search for Self in the Revolutionary Era* (Princeton University Press, 2002).

8 Fletcher, *William Edmondson: A Retrospective*, 186, fig. 48a.

Lee Godie

1 Alex Wald, cited in Michael Bonesteel, "Lee Godie: Art and Survival on the Streets of Chicago," in *Artist—Lee Godie: A 20-Year Retrospective*, exh. cat. (City of Chicago Department of Cultural Affairs, 1993), 10. Wald is speaking of 1968, at the very start of Godie's art career, when Wald worked in the Art Institute bookstore and Godie was selling her paintings in front of the museum.

2 Valérie Rousseau, "Actions photographiques ou La formulation de l'alter ego," in Bruno Decharme, ed., *Photo Brut: Collection Bruno Decharme & Compagnie* (Flammarion, 2019), 176–77.

3 Bonesteel, "Lee Godie: Art and Survival on the Streets of Chicago," in Bonesteel, *Artist—Lee Godie*, 10–11.

4 See Jessica Moss, *Lee Godie: Finding Beauty*, exh. cat. (Intuit Art Museum, 2008), n.p. The quotes and details that follow are all taken from this publication.

Jesse Howard

1 C. J. Janovy, "Ornery Artist's Hand-Lettered Screeds Helped Him Keep the World at Bay," KCUR, Feb. 8, 2015, https://www.npr.org/2015/02/08/384128399/ornery-artist-s-hand-lettered-screeds-helped-him-keep-the-world-at-bay.

2 Gregg N. Blasdel, "The Grass-Roots Artist," *Art in America* 56 (Sept. 1, 1968): 24, 26.

3 Ben stated this idea several times over the course of his life. For example, see Andres Pardey and Ben Vautier, *Tout est art ? Ben*, exh. cat. (Musée Maillol, 2016).

4 Lynne Cooke, ed., *Outliers and American Vanguard Art*, exh. cat. (National Gallery of Art, 2018), is among the more thorough and widely recognized of these endeavors. See also Colin Rhodes, *Outsider Art: Spontaneous Alternatives* (Thames and Hudson, 2000); Gary Alan Fine, *Everyday Genius: Self-Taught Art and the Culture of Authenticity* (University of Chicago Press, 2004); and Kerry James Marshall, "The Beatitudes of Bill Traylor," in *Between Worlds: The Art of Bill Traylor*, ed. Leslie Umberger, exh. cat. (Smithsonian American Art Museum, 2018), 25–29.

Annette Messager

1 Annette Messager, *Les Tortures Volontaires/Voluntary Tortures* (Hatje Cantz, 2012).

2 *Les Tortures Volontaires* has *Album-Collection No. 18* as a subtitle; it is one of fifty-six such photo-albums created by Messager between 1971 and 1974, the first of which is titled *The Marriage of Miss Annette Messager*. See Sheryl Conkelton and Carol S. Eliel, *Annette Messager*, exh. cat. (Los Angeles County Museum of Art; Museum of Modern Art, 1995), 12.

Mr. Imagination

1 Tom Patterson, "Mr. Imagination, Gregory Warmack (1948–2012)," *Raw Vision*, Obituaries, accessed Aug. 27, 2025, https://rawvision.com/blogs/obituaries/news-gregory-warmack-aka-mr-imagination-1948-e2-80-93-2012.

2 "Mr. Imagination/Gregory Warmack," Carl Hammer Gallery, accessed Aug. 27, 2025, https://www.carlhammergallery.com/artists/mr-imagination-gregory-warmack (site discontinued).

3 Mary Houlihan, "Folk artist Gregory Warmack, aka Mr. Imagination, saw art in any object," *Chicago Tribune*, May 30, 2012, updated Dec. 24, 2018, https://www.chicago-tribune.com/2012/05/31/folk-artist-gregory-warmack-aka-mr-imagination-saw-art-in-any-object-2/. A similar photograph can be seen in Tom Patterson's obituary for *Raw Vision*.

4 "Mr. Imagination/Gregory Warmack," Carl Hammer Gallery.

5 Kristin Otto, "Shapes of the Ancestors: Bodies, Animals, Art, and Ghanaian Fantasy Coffins," *Museum Anthropology Review* 13, no. 1–2 (Mar. 2019): 49.

Martín Ramírez

1 Víctor M. Espinosa, *Martín Ramírez: Framing His Life and Art* (University of Texas Press, 2015). The following excerpt is taken from the introduction, pp. 1–12, with minor edits for clarity.

Cindy Sherman

1 See Gabriele Schor, ed., *Cindy Sherman: The Early Works 1975–1977: Catalogue Raisonné* (Hatje Cantz, 2012), 61–66, 164–213. *A Play of Selves* was installed in Buffalo in August 1976 at *Open Spaces*, an exhibition at the artist-run gallery Hallwalls; Sherman's longtime gallery Metro Pictures presented it for the second time in 2006 (Schor, 66).

2 Cindy Sherman in conversation with Gabriele Schor, July 2010, cited in Schor, *Cindy Sherman: The Early Works*, 37.

3 Schor, 37. The catalogue raisonné includes a number of photobooth pictures, which artist and Hallwalls administrator Michael Zwack enabled by renting a machine for the purpose.

4 Schor, 14–15.

5 Betsy Berne, "Parallel Lives," in *Cindy Sherman 2016* (Hartmann Books, 2016), 46.

6 Blake Gopnik, "Ready for Her Close-Up," *The New York Times* (Apr. 24, 2016): AR1, AR18.

7 Richard Adler, "*I Love Lucy* Dominates Television Comedy," ebsco.com, 2023, https://www.ebsco.com/research-starters/arts-and-entertainment/i-love-lucy-dominates-television-comedy.

8 The show had apparently grown so popular that, per Adler, "*I Love Lucy* Dominates Television Comedy," Marshall Field's department store in Chicago changed its late hours from Monday to Thursday so as not to conflict with the show's slot on Mondays at 9 p.m. Eastern time. Adler further relates that in 1962, Ball bought out Arnaz's share in Desilu Productions, selling the company five years later to Gulf and Western for $17 million.

Bill Traylor

1 For an extended comparison, see Josef Helfenstein and Roxanne Stanulis, eds., *Bill Traylor, William Edmondson, and the Modernist Impulse*, exh. cat. (Krannert Art Museum, University of Illinois, 2004).

2 Umberger, *Between Worlds: The Art of Bill Traylor*.

3 Josef Helfenstein, "From the Sidewalk to the Marketplace: Traylor, Edmondson, and the Modernist Impulse," in Helfenstein and Stanulis, 58.

4 Charles Shannon, "Bill Traylor's Triumph," *Art and Antiques* 11, no. 2 (Feb. 1988): 64, cited in Helfenstein, 53.

5 Umberger, relying on period accounts but also on extended examination of the drawings, builds a convincing stylistic chronology in the second part of her monograph.

6 See Margaret Lynne Ausfeld, "'A World unto Itself': Bill Traylor's Montgomery," in Helfenstein and Stanulis, 87–93.

7 Helfenstein, 60.

8 Umberger, 110–11.

9 Helfenstein, 62.

Eugene Von Bruenchenhein

1 Joanne Cubbs, "Eugene Von Bruenchenhein: Obsessive Visionary," in *Eugene Von Bruenchenhein: Obsessive Visionary*, exh. cat. (John Michael Kohler Arts Center, 1988), 11. Von Bruenchenhein affixed the phrase "Create and be recognized" to a basement wall in his home. The Kohler Arts Center took over a significant portion of Von Bruenchenhein's estate following his death in 1983. Cubbs, who organized the 1988 exhibition, consulted the artist's extensive diaries and tape recordings (likewise held at the Kohler Center) and, in 1983 to 1984, interviewed the artist's widow and two others close to him.

2 Cubbs (1988), 19; see also Joanne Cubbs, *Eugene Von Bruenchenhein: King of Lesser Lands*, exh. cat. (Andrew Edlin Gallery, 2016), 14–47.

3 Cubbs (1988), 19.

4 Cubbs (2016), 7.

Kara Walker

1 Rebecca Peabody, *Consuming Stories: Kara Walker and the Imagining of American Race* (University of California Press, 2005).

2 Cooke, *Outliers and American Vanguard Art.* See in particular Thomas J. Lax, "Museums, oh Museums," 81; Cooke, "Boundary Trouble: Navigating Margin and Mainstream," 20–23. Cooke cited Anne M. Wagner, *Three Artists (Three Women): Modernism and the Art of Hesse, Krasner, and O'Keeffe* (University of California Press, 1996) for the phrase "difference determines differently," which she alters slightly to yield "determine difference differently."

3 Email communication with Allison Calhoun, Kara Walker Studio, May 14, 2025. Calhoun relayed that Walker made some works on glass in graduate school (Rhode Island School of Design, 1991–94) and that she considers these mirrors "typical of the times."

4 In addition to the example of *Harper's Pictorial History of the Civil War*, Walker recently disfigured and reconfigured a 1921 bronze statue of Civil War general Thomas J. "Stonewall" Jackson — titling the reworked memorial *Unmanned Drone* — as a key contribution to the exhibition *Monuments*, co-organized by the Museum of Contemporary Art, Los Angeles, and The Brick, Los Angeles, from October 23, 2025, to May 3, 2026.

5 The exhibition catalogue *A Black Hole is Everything a Star Longs to Be: Drawings 1992–2020*, ed. Anita Haldemann (JRP Ringier, 2020), contains a rich sampling of each of these strategies. For *Harper's Pictorial History…* see Cooke, 320–23.

6 See the Paul Collins website, https://www.collinsart.org/, which includes a digital booklet in which Collins "identifies as Black and multiracial" and emphasizes the need to overcome bigotry and racism through depictions of harmonious community.

7 Email communication with Kara Walker Studio, May 14, 2025.

8 "Black Folk Art Redux: A Curatorial Roundtable," in Cooke, 77. Beardsley co-curated, with Jane Livingston, the landmark exhibition *Black Folk Art in America 1930–1980* (Corcoran Gallery of Art, 1980). He cites as influential for his disambiguation of the terms "vernacular," "popular," and "mass," an essay by Christopher Lasch, "Mass Culture Reconsidered," *Democracy* (Oct. 1981): 7–22.

Slim Wasson

1 "Well-Known Upper Pecos Resident Dies," *Santa Fe New Mexican*, Sunday Edition, May 17, 1962, 6, NewspaperArchive.com. New Mexico gained statehood in 1912. The ancestry website FamilySearch lists Wasson among eleven siblings and notes that his younger brother Samuel Franklin Wasson was born in Wagon Mound, Mora County, New Mexico. Rather than relocating there, Slim Wasson may simply have been born in New Mexico as well. See "Arthur R 'Slim' Wasson," FamilySearch.com, last updated Apr. 16, 2023, https://www.familysearch.org/en/tree/person/details/GKNT-118.

2 Findagrave.com includes an image of Wasson's grave in Fairview Cemetery in Santa Fe, which includes a modestly decorated headstone that gives only his name and life dates.

3 For more on Austin, see Kathy Weiser-Alexander and David Alexander, "Forked Lightning Ranch, New Mexico," Legends of America, last updated Mar. 2025, accessed Aug. 27, 2025, https://www.legendsofamerica.com/forked-lightning-ranch-new-mexico/. See also "Tex Austin," Pecos National Historical Park, New Mexico, last updated May 8, 2020, https://www.nps.gov/peco/learn/historyculture/tex-austin.htm. Perusing these colorful websites yields the news that Austin probably was born in 1889, in Missouri, as Clarence Van Norstrand; evidently possessed of outsized ambitions, he operated rodeo events in Albuquerque, Wichita, New York, Chicago, and London from 1916 to 1932. The largest of these events, lasting nine days, attracted 350,000 customers to Soldier Field in Chicago, in 1927.

4 See Weiser-Alexander and Alexander, "Forked Lightning Ranch, New Mexico," and "Tex Austin," National Historic Park of New Mexico.

5 Georgia O'Keeffe signed her name in the ranch's guest book, now in the Pecos National Historical Park archives, on August 6, 1968. See also "The Forked Lightning Ranch," Pecos National Historical Park, New Mexico, last updated Jan. 22, 2021, accessed Aug. 27, 2025, https://www.nps.gov/peco/learn/historyculture/the-forked-lightning-ranch.htm. Actress and activist Jane Fonda later purchased some of the ranch's land.

6 Mrs. E. E. Fogelson (Greer Garson), "Biographical Notes on Arthur L. (Slim) Wasson," Pecos National Historical Park, New Mexico, file PECO-00120. All subsequent quotes by Garson are from this document, kindly supplied by Janine Fron on behalf of Richard and Ellen Sandor. The Sandors were drawn to this work by Wasson in part because of Garson's role in his story and in the history of the ranch.

7 The Sandors and I thank Rhonda Brewer, museum curator at the Pecos National Historical Park, for sharing these images.

8 Cori Knudten and Maren Bzdek, *Crossroads of Change: An Environmental History of Pecos National Historical Park*, vol. 2 (Public Lands History Center, Colorado State University, Aug. 2010), 106–15.

9 Knudten and Bzdek, 128, 146.

10 Ted Faye, "Of Myths and Men: Separating Fact from Fiction in the Twenty Mule Team Story," *Borax Pioneer* 17 (U.S. Borax, Inc., 1999), https://scvhistory.com/scvhistory/borax1799.htm.

11 "History of the U.S. Borax 20 Mule Team," U.S. Borax, accessed Aug. 27, 2025, https://www.borax.com/about/history.

Joseph E. Yoakum

1 Mark Pascale, Esther Adler, and Édouard Kopp, eds., *Joseph E. Yoakum: What I Saw*, exh. cat. (Art Institute of Chicago, 2021). The exhibition was co-organized with the Museum of Modern Art and the Menil Collection.

2 For "two thousand drawings," see Whitney Halstead, "Joseph E. Yoakum," manuscript from 1975, published in Pascale et al., 209.

3 Pascale, "Revisiting Joseph E. Yoakum's Chicago Legacy," in Pascale et al., 17–18. See also Thea Liberty Nichols, Mark Pascale, and Ann Goldstein, eds., *Hairy Who? 1966–1969*, exh. cat. (Art Institute of Chicago, 2018); and Thea Liberty Nichols and Mark Pascale, eds., *Christina Ramberg: A Retrospective*, exh. cat. (Art Institute of Chicago, 2024). Pascale's earlier exhibitions on artists as varied as Charles White, Eldzier Cortor, and James Castle are equally pertinent.

4 Folsom, California, Candy Store Gallery, *Three Famous Artists: Gladys Nilsson, Joseph Yoakum, and Jim Nutt*, Nov. 16–Dec. 31, 1969, no cat.

5 Cooke, "Black Folk Art Redux," in *Outliers and American Vanguard Art*, 77. The exhibition was held in early 1994 at one or two university galleries in Tennessee.

6 Halstead, 209.

7 Emily Olek, "The Fantastical Reality of Joseph E. Yoakum: A Chronology," in Pascale et al., 28; and Laura K. Minton, "Paging through Places," in Pascale et al., 80. A mention of J. A. Brimm & Sons Hardware Store in Walnut Grove appears in *Talking Machine and Radio Weekly* 29, no. 16 (Apr. 16, 1930): 18, https://www.worldradiohistory.com/Archive-Talking-Machine-Radio-Weekly/TMRW1930-04-16.pdf.

8 Esther Adler, "Unfolding Joseph E. Yoakum: Christian Science and Life on the South Side," in Pascale et al., 45–55. See also Guillaume Olivier, "La science chrétienne de Mary Baker Eddy: Une religion de la contradiction?" (PhD diss., École Pratique des Hautes Études, 2024). For more on Eddy's influence on artists, see for example Marci Kwon, *Enchantments: Joseph Cornell and American Modernism* (Princeton University Press, 2021), 7–8.

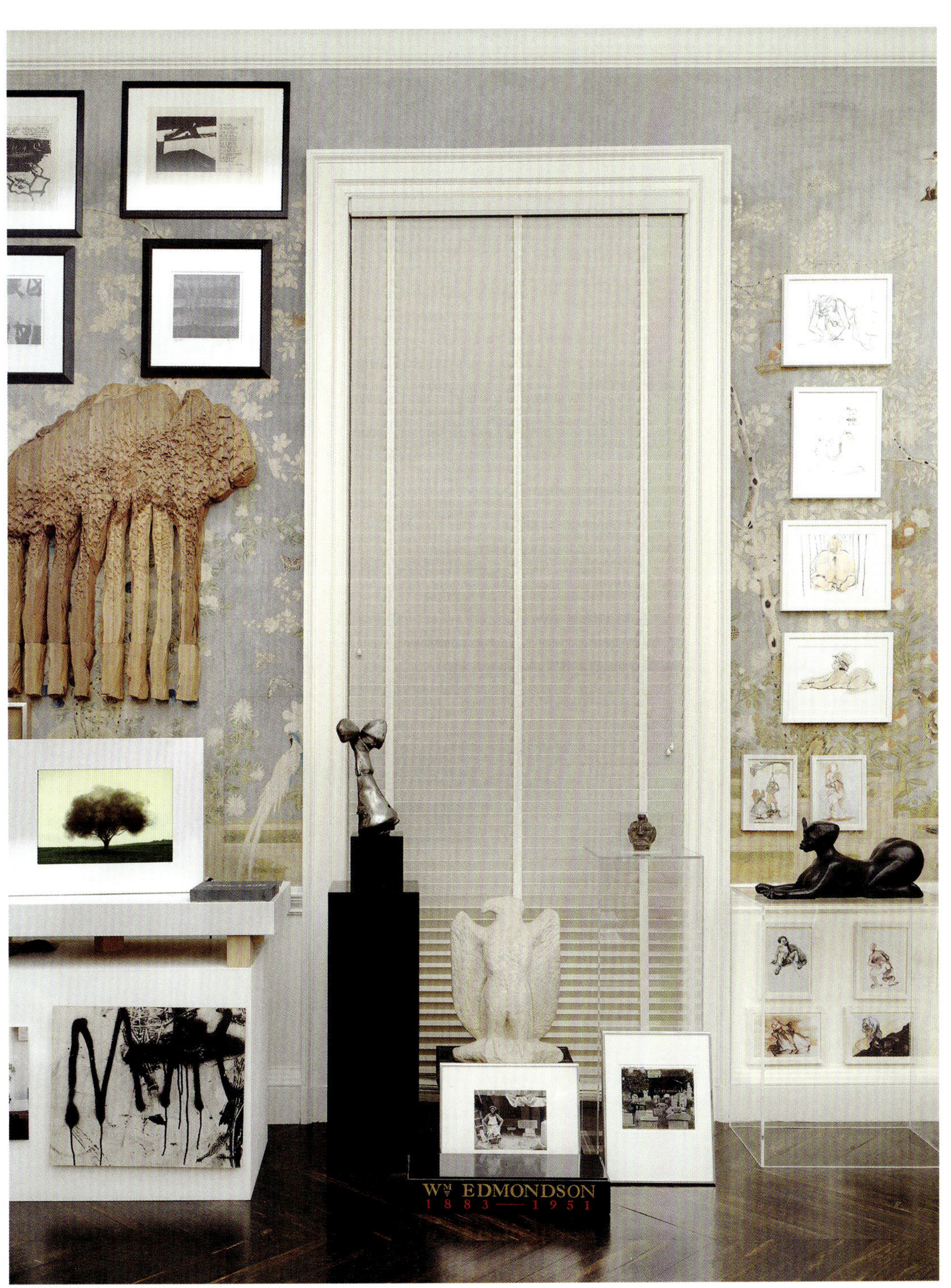
Wm EDMONDSON
1883—1951

Checklist of Gift

All works are in the collection of the Art Institute of Chicago and are gifts of Richard and Ellen Sandor.

Titles of works derive from their inscriptions and aim to preserve artists' spellings.

(art)^{n}
Founded Chicago, 1983

Ellen Sandor
Born Brooklyn, NY, 1942; active Chicago

James Zanzi
Born Chicago, 1940; active Chicago

The Other Window: Distortion I '06
2006
Computer-interleaved Duratrans and Kodalith
62.3 × 52.1 × 7 cm (24 ½ × 20 ½ × 2 ¾ in.)
2025.871
Frontispiece

Eddie Arning
Born Germania, TX, 1898; died McGregor, TX, 1993

Kodak Makes Your Pictures Count
1970–73
Oil pastel on paper
50.5 × 65.2 cm (19 15⁄16 × 25 11⁄16 in.)
2025.997.1
Pl. 1

Kodak Makes Your Pictures Count
1970–73
Published by Eastman Kodak Company (founded Rochester, NY, c. 1888)
Printed matter
33.5 × 53 cm (13 ¼ × 20 ⅞ in.)
2025.997.2
P. 29, fig. 1

William Edmondson
Born Davidson County, TN, 1874; died Nashville, 1951

Eagle
c. 1940s
Limestone
56.6 × 39.4 × 18.5 cm (22 ¼ × 15 ½ × 7 ¼ in.)
2025.611
Pl. 3

Lee Godie
Born Chicago, 1908; died Plato Center, IL, 1994

Lee — I Kept Saying Left Side and Grooves till I Got to the Camera Sincerily
1970s
Gelatin silver print
12.1 × 9.6 cm (4 ¾ × 3 ¾ in.)
2025.872
Pl. 4

Lee and Cameo on a Chair Sincerily Lee Godie
1970s
Gelatin silver print with ink
12.1 × 9.6 cm (4 ¾ × 3 ¾ in.)
2025.873
Pl. 5

This Is a News Front Page Picture …
1970s
Gelatin silver print with ink
12.1 × 9.6 cm (4 ¾ × 3 ¾ in.)
2025.874
Pl. 6

Lee — When My Coat Was New Sincerily
1970s
Gelatin silver print with ink
12.1 × 9.6 cm (4 ¾ × 3 ¾ in.)
2025.875
Pl. 7

Hands
1980s
Watercolor, ballpoint pen, and graphite on canvas
45.5 × 129.5 cm (17 15⁄16 × 51 in.)
2025.1001
Pl. 8

Daisies White and Orange
1970s–80s
Watercolor and ballpoint pen on canvas
58.4 × 46 cm (23 × 18 ⅛ in.)
2025.998
Pl. 9

Profile Portrait
1970s–80s
Paint and ballpoint pen with graphite on canvas sewn to synthetic fabric
65.5 × 47.5 cm (25 13⁄16 × 18 ¾ in.)
2025.999
Pl. 10

Be My Valentine
1970s–80s
Paint and ballpoint pen on canvas
60.7 × 91 cm (23 15⁄16 × 35 ⅞ in.)
2025.1000
Pl. 11

Jesse Howard
Born Shamrock Township, MO, 1885; died Fulton, MO, 1983

Untitled (Quote Behold How Good . . .)
1953–71
Paint on wood with found windmill wheel assembly and pipe
73.7 × 68.6 × 114.3 cm (29 × 27 × 45 in.)
2025.617
Pl. 12

Untitled (And I Will Give Unto Thee . . .)
Nov. 11, 1976
Sign: paint and graphite on hardboard; key: paint on hardboard
Overall: 53.4 × 61 × 2.6 cm (21 × 24 × 1 in.); sign: 25.4 × 50.8 × 0.4 cm (10 × 20 × ⅛ in.); key: 10.7 × 40.7 × 0.4 cm (4 3⁄16 × 16 × ⅛ in.)
2025.612
Pl. 13

Untitled (St. Louis Globe. Fri. Dec. 30. 1960)
Jan. 30, 1962
Paint and graphite on metal
50.8 × 65.1 × 0.4 cm (20 × 25 ⅝ × ⅛ in.)
2025.616
Pl. 14

Untitled (Angry, And Temper Causes Boy To Loose His Life . . .)
1953–83
Paint and graphite on wood
25.1 × 134 cm (9 ⅞ × 52 ¾ in.)
2025.613
Pl. 15

Untitled (Brain Washed Yesser . . .)
1953–71
Paint on wood
28.3 × 342.9 × 3.9 cm (11 ⅛ × 135 × 1 ½ in.)
2025.614
Pl. 16

The Thorn Tree
1968
Paint and graphite on canvas with wood dowel
91.5 × 113.1 × 2 cm (36 × 44 ½ × ¾ in.)
2025.618
Pl. 17

Man's Best Friend
Feb. 18, 1974
Paint and graphite on canvas with wood dowel
122 × 88.6 × 2.6 cm (48 × 34 ⅞ × 1 in.)
2025.619
Pl. 18

Untitled (Corruption. Did You Ever See A Ball Of Maggots . . .)
1953–83
Paint on wood
11.5 × 149.9 cm (4 ½ × 59 in.)
2025.615
Pl. 20

Annette Messager
Born Berck, France, 1943; active Paris

Les Tortures Volontaires (Voluntary Tortures): Album-Collection No. 18
1972
83 gelatin silver prints
Installation dimensions variable
2025.876.1–83
Pl. 21

Mr. Imagination
Born Chicago, 1948; died Atlanta, 2012

Bottlecap Fish
2002
Found aluminum bottle caps and acrylic on plaster, wood, and tin
21.6 × 29.3 × 10.8 cm (8 ½ × 11 ½ × 4 ¼ in.)
2025.620
Pl. 22

Martín Ramírez
Born Jalisco, Mexico, 1895; died Auburn, CA, 1963

Untitled (Jinete with Red Shirt No. 3)
1950–55
Graphite, tempera, and crayon on 2 sheets of cream wove paper, pieced
72.5 × 61 cm (28 9⁄16 × 24 1⁄16 in.)
2025.1002
Pl. 23

Cindy Sherman
Born Glen Ridge, NJ, 1954; active New York

Untitled (Lucy)
1975, printed 2001
Chromogenic print
25.4 × 20.4 cm (10 × 8 in.)
2025.877
Pl. 24

Bill Traylor
Born Benton, AL, c. 1853; died Montgomery, 1949

Untitled (Two Figures, Female Figure Pointing)
1939–42
Graphite and opaque water-color on brown cardboard
38.2 × 33.3 cm (15 1⁄16 × 13 ⅛ in.)
2025.1003
Pl. 26

Eugene Von Bruenchenhein
Born Marinette, WI, 1910; died Milwaukee, WI, 1983

Untitled
1940s–50s
Gelatin silver print with applied letters
29.9 × 24.8 cm (11 ¾ × 9 ¾ in.)
2025.881
Pl. 27

Untitled
1940s–50s
Gelatin silver print
12.7 × 17.8 cm (5 × 7 in.)
2025.882
Pl. 28

Untitled
1940s–50s
Gelatin silver print
12.7 × 17.8 cm (5 × 7 in.)
2025.884
Pl. 29

Untitled
1940s–50s
Gelatin silver print
12.7 × 17.8 cm (5 × 7 in.)
2025.883
Pl. 30

Untitled
1940s–50s
Gelatin silver print
20.4 × 25.4 cm (8 × 10 in.)
2025.879
Pl. 31

Untitled
1940s–50s
Gelatin silver print
25.4 × 20.4 cm (10 × 8 in.)
2025.880
Pl. 32

Untitled
1940s–50s
Gelatin silver print
25.1 × 17.8 cm (9 7/8 × 7 in.)
2025.885
Pl. 33

Untitled
1940s–50s
Gelatin silver print
21 × 18.5 cm (8 1/4 × 7 1/4 in.)
2025.878

Kara Walker
Born Stockton, CA, 1969; active New York

Free, Black, and Passive Aggressive
1998
Ink and paint on 16 found objects
Overall: 123.2 × 508 cm (48 1/2 × 200 in.)
2025.750a–p
Pl. 34

Slim Wasson
Born 1881; died Santa Fe, 1962

Twenty Mule Team
c. 1961
Painted wood, leather, metal wire and hardware, rubber, and cotton
43.2 × 32.1 × 461.1 cm (17 × 12 5/8 × 181 1/2 in.)
2025.621
Pl. 35

John Waters
Born Baltimore, 1946; active Baltimore

Sequel
1995
Chromogenic print
18.4 × 213.4 × 2.5 cm (7 1/4 × 84 × 1 in.) (framed)
2025.886
Pl. 37

Edward Weston
Born Highland Park, IL, 1886; died Carmel Highlands, CA, 1958

William Edmondson, Sculptor
1941
Gelatin silver print
19.1 × 24.1 cm (7 1/2 × 9 1/2 in.)
2025.889
P. 35, fig. 1

Carvings of William Edmondson of Nashville
1941
Gelatin silver print
19.1 × 24.1 cm (7 1/2 × 9 1/2 in.)
2025.888
P. 35, fig. 2

László Willinger
Born Budapest, 1909; died Los Angeles, 1989

Lucille Ball
c. 1950
Gelatin silver print
24.2 × 18.8 cm (9 9/16 × 7 3/8 in.)
2025.887
P. 73, fig. 1

Joseph E. Yoakum
Born Ash Grove, MO, 1891; died Rock Island, IL, 1972

The Mounds of Pleasure on J.A. Brimms Farm near Walnut Grove Missouri
Mar. 7, 1970
Ink and pastel on white wove paper
39.5 × 30 cm (15 9/16 × 11 13/16 in.)
2025.1008
Pl. 40

Holland Tunnal in Adirondack Mtn Range near Albany New York
n.d.
Ink and pastel on white wove paper
30.3 × 48.4 cm (11 15/16 × 19 1/16 in.)
2025.1007
Pl. 41

Nat King Cole Roveing Comedian & Entertainer Age & Birth Place Not Sure
Apr. 4, 1963
Ink, graphite, and crayon on cream wove paper
45.1 × 30.2 cm (17 3/4 × 11 7/8 in.)
2025.1006
Pl. 42

Mt. Brigham, Along Continental Divid near Tryslu Alberta Canada North of North Western Montana
n.d.
Ink and pastel on white wove paper
30.5 × 45.8 cm (12 × 18 in.)
2025.1004
Pl. 43

Great Dividing Range of Queensland Sector near Brisbane Australia
June 3, 1963
Ink and pastel on paper
30.5 × 45.8 cm (12 × 18 in.)
2025.1005
Pl. 44

Photography Credits

Unless otherwise noted, photographs of artworks in the collection of the Art Institute of Chicago are copyrighted by the Art Institute of Chicago.

Photographs of artworks in the collection of the Art Institute of Chicago are by Nathan Keay, Robert Lifson, Jonathan Mathias, Juan Molina Hérnandez, and Joe Tallarico, with postproduction by Kaitlyn Fultz-Campion and Hayley Hinsberger.

The Art Institute of Chicago makes reasonable efforts to identify and contact copyright holders when necessary, but also asserts its fair use rights in the reproduction of applicable illustrations in its publications. We adhere to the standards set by the Association of Art Museum Directors' Guidelines for the Use of Copyrighted Materials and Works of Art by Art Museums. We make every reasonable attempt to ensure the accuracy of credit and caption information for each image. Any uncredited creators or rights holders are encouraged to contact the Art Institute of Chicago. The following credits apply to all images in this book for which separate acknowledgment is due.

P. 11: Richard and Ellen Sandor, Chicago, 2025; p. 16, fig. 3; p. 20, fig. 5; p. 24, fig. 7; p. 123: The Sandor family apartment. Photos by Jamie Stukenberg.

P. 13, fig. 1: © Walker Evans Archive, The Metropolitan Museum of Art.

P. 14, fig. 2; p. 23, fig. 6: Photos by Herb Booth Studio Inc.

P. 19, fig. 4: Photo by Jamie Stukenberg. Image by E. J. Bellocq © Lee Friedlander, courtesy of Fraenkel Gallery, San Francisco.

P. 30, fig. 2: Digital Image © The Museum of Modern Art / Licensed by SCALA / Art Resource, NY. © 2026 Wyeth Foundation for American Art / Artists Rights Society (ARS), New York.

P. 33, pl. 2; p. 59, pl. 19; p. 65, fig. 1; pp. 106–7, pls. 36–37; p. 109, pl. 39: Imaging, the Art Institute of Chicago.

P. 35, figs. 1–2: Photograph by Edward Weston © Center for Creative Photography, Arizona Board of Regents.

P. 50, fig. 1: Photo by Philippe Migeat, Christian Bahier. Digital Image © CNAC / MNAM, Dist. RMN-Grand Palais / Art Resource, NY. © 2026 Ben Vautier / Artists Rights Society (ARS), New York / ADAGP, Paris.

Pp. 62–63, pl. 21: © 2026 Artists Rights Society (ARS), New York / ADAGP, Paris.

P. 71, pl. 23: © Estate of Martín Ramírez.

P. 75, pl. 24; p. 77, pl. 25: © 2026 Cindy Sherman / Artists Rights Society (ARS), NY. Courtesy of the artist and Hauser & Wirth.

P. 81, pl. 26: Used with permission from Artistry of Bill Traylor, LLC and Bill Traylor Family Trust.

P. 83, fig. 1: Photo courtesy of John Michael Kohler Arts Center.

Pp. 95–97, pl. 35: © Kara Walker.

Pp. 106–9, pls. 36–39: © John Waters. Courtesy of the artist and Marianne Boesky Gallery, New York and Aspen.

Self, Made: Fourteen Modern Artists from the Richard and Ellen Sandor Family Collection was published in conjunction with an exhibition of the same title organized by the Art Institute of Chicago from June 27 through November 9, 2026.

First edition
Printed in Turkey
30 29 28 27 26 1 2 3 4 5

Authorized representative in the EU: Easy Access System Europe, Mustamäe tee 50, 10621 Tallinn, Estonia, gpsr.requests @easproject.com

ISBN: 978-0-300-28855-1 (hardcover)

Library of Congress Control Number: 2026934000

Published by
The Art Institute of Chicago
111 South Michigan Avenue
Chicago, IL 60603-6404
artic.edu

Distributed by
Yale University Press
302 Temple Street
P. O. Box 209040
New Haven, CT 06520-9040
yalebooks.com/art

Edited by Nora McGreevy
Production by David Khan-Giordano
Photography research by Kristie Kahns
Proofreading by David Olsen
Design and typesetting by Studio Blue
Separations by Professional Graphics, Rockford, Illinois
Printing and binding by Ofset Yapimevi, Istanbul

Publishing, the Art Institute of Chicago
Katie Reilly, Associate Vice President, Publishing
Lisa Meyerowitz, Editorial Director
Lauren Makholm, Director of Production

Imaging, the Art Institute of Chicago
Bonnie Rosenberg, Director of Imaging
Nathan Keay, Associate Director, Photography
Elyse M. Allen, Associate Director, Production

This book is typeset in Caslon 540 by Bitstream and Neue Haas Unica by Linotype. Caslon was used to print the Declaration of Independence and the plainspoken, eloquent first edition of *Walker Evans: American Photographs* (1938); in the late 1920s or early 1930s, Chicago's Ludlow Typograph Company also produced a version called Caslon True Cut. Although Ludlow's type was never digitized, Bitstream's cut closely recalls the typeface's distinctive Chicago variant.

Cover: Lee Godie, *Lee and Cameo on a Chair Sincerily Lee Godie*, 1970s (pl. 5). Photo by Juan Molina Hernández.

Frontispiece: (art)^n, Ellen Sandor, and James Zanzi, *The Other Window: Distortion I '06*, 2006.

This book was made using paper and materials certified by the Forest Stewardship Council, which ensures responsible forest management.

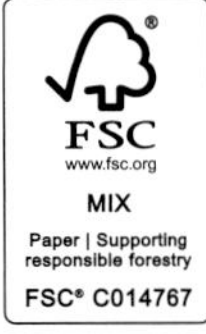